Who Touched Me?

My Journey To Jesus

Tron Moses

Copyright © 2017 by Tron Moses.

All rights reserved
Rejoice Essential Publishing
P.O. BOX 85
Bennettsville, SC 29512
www.republishing.org

All rights reserved. No part of this book may be used or reproduced by any means, graphic, electronic, or mechanical, including photocopying, recording, taping or by any information storage retrieval system without the written permission of the publisher except in the case of brief quotations embodied in critical articles and reviews.

Visit the author's website at www.tronmoses.org

While the author has made every effort to provide accurate internet addresses at the time of publication, neither the publisher nor the author assumes any responsibility for errors or for changes that occur after publication.

Who Touched Me? My Journey To Jesus/Tron Moses

ISBN-10: 1-946756-06-7
ISBN-13: 978-1-946756-06-0

Library of Congress Control Number: 2017942305

We overcome by the blood of the lamb and by the word of our testimony. In this book I take you on a journey with me and speak to you as if you were sitting across from me. I show you the good and the bad. I show you how I walked away from the Father and ran for 10 years until I found my way back home. I was the Prodigal Son, and this is my story.

"I give this book 5 stars because it is an excellent book telling the importance of one man's journey to our King Jesus" ~ Stephanie~

"Just finished this book, this is proof that the Lord has no respect of persons. It's proof of the Glory, Grace, and Mercy of the Lord. It doesn't matter your background, faults, or hang-ups; the Lord will use your tragedy and turn it into Ministry for a testimony of His Love" ~ LaTasha Moses ~

"This is an awesome book showing how God can use and deliver anyone from evil. It's going to be a blessing to a lot of people" ~ Marcus Ford ~

Contents

Foreword vii

In The Beginning 1

Summertime In SC 4

Public School 25 7

Lexington Avenue 14

Fulton Street 29

South Carolina Vacation 35

Back On L.E.X. Again 40

Moving Down South 59

Moving To North Carolina 64

My Appointed Time 75

God's Hand Of Protection 84

Foreword

When I first picked up the copy of the book, "Who Touched Me" by Tron Moses, I was hooked. I couldn't put the book down. I read the whole book in one day. I was always curious about who he was and his life story. I would see Tron Moses on YouTube and he seemed so mysterious. I couldn't believe what I read inside of this beautiful book. God has truly done a great work in the life of Tron Moses. I could see Tron's heart and the wisdom that he carried. Tron narrates a thrilling journey of his childhood, his life, his hardships, his fears, his accomplishments, and best of all, how he converted from the power of darkness into God's marvelous light. He lived a hard life but the Lord blessed him with so many talents. As I read each page, I could feel Tron's pain and gained a deeper understanding of his life and his testimony. When I read about some of the things Tron endured I could feel the tears forming. I have been blessed to know Tron on a personal level and we have developed a beautiful friendship. He has been there for my hardships and encouraged me along the way. Tron is a man of faith and he is very grateful for the gift of life.

Tron Moses is my soon to be husband, my photographer, and my partner for the magazine, "Rejoice Essential." He is a true man of God and practices what He preaches. I can attest that the Tron inside the book is the selfless Tron that we know in the body of Christ. I admire Tron in so many ways, I watch him on a daily basis helping and blessing others on the platform God gave him. I could relate to "Who Touched Me" in many ways. I was a victim of abuse and a culprit of it. I was scorned, bitter, depressed, and I lived a fast that was full of drugs, sex, and hustling until I almost died in 2004. This is when I became saved. I gave up exotic dancing and followed after God. When I read this book, I felt so much closer to Tron and could see my life in so many ways in his story.

As an established author of over a dozen books, with my own publishing company, I highly recommend this book to people from all walks of life. People need to know that there is a better way, and a life of sin and violence isn't it. I truly believe that the world needs to hear this story because the anointing that's on it will save many souls by planting seeds of the gospel and introduce them to Jesus Christ. There are many praying mothers, fathers, grandparents, brothers, and sisters who are believing God to save your loved ones. After you read the story that unfolds in this book, you will have the faith to believe for their salvation.

Author Kimberly Hargraves
Rejoice Essential Publishing, LLC.
Founder and Chief Editor, Rejoice Essential Magazine.

CHAPTER ONE

In The Beginning

Me, my sister, and my mother were running down the stairs from our third floor apartment; I remember it like it was yesterday. My sister was 5 years old, and I was 3 years old. My mother had my sister on her left and me on her right. She had my left hand and with my right hand I was holding up my pants because I didn't have a belt on and they were falling. There was a man behind us chasing us and I kept looking back at him. He was too close to us not to grab us. All my life it puzzled me as to why this guy was chasing us, but we'll get back to that later.

I was born 1975 in Brooklyn Jewish hospital to Mary Moses and Jimmy Larkins. Life was pretty decent growing up. We didn't have everything we wanted, but we had what we needed, each other. My mother worked hard to support her family; I've always known her to work. We lived in Brooklyn, NY and our big brother was being raised in Blenheim, SC. My mother use to have her little afro and bell-bottoms. She had a big music collection: Al Green, The Temptations, The Whisperers, Teddy Pendergrass, Barry White, Earth Wind, & Fire! So she would be jamming around the house listening to her soul and disco. We were raised in a single parent home and would see our father maybe once or twice a year. I loved his style even though I barely knew him. He was always stylish; the man was dressed to impress. He would have a suit on, nice shoes, shirt opened up enough to show his chest hairs and a tilted brim, straight out the 70s.

My mother and father's relationship didn't work out because pops was a player. He had already left us while I was still a newborn baby and had a baby with another woman the following year. We lived in East New York, a rough section in Brooklyn. I remember playing outside with cousins and having a great time in the 70s. I was too young at the time to understand the importance of having family around. A lot of people grew up with large families, spending the night, coming to visit regularly, and in some cases living together. I don't recall living in East New York too long. My mother worked at the telephone company and they went on a strike. Next thing I know we was living in the projects in Brownsville, another rough section in Brooklyn. We stayed with a friend of my mother and her two daughters. I loved it over there; I was like 4 years old and loved to play outside on the monkey bars. Even at that young age I knew we were living in a dangerous area. One day the two sisters, Mookie & Davida, had a cousin over and the cousin didn't like my sister. So Mookie & Davida instigated a fight between the two, but this was the strangest fight I've ever seen. They gave my sister and their cousin a pen each, so they could stab each other. My sister (Tasha) always had heart, she would never back down. I stood there just watching while they stabbed one another with ink pens.

I was 4, my sister was 6, and I think Mookie & Davida was like 8 and 9. I had a little crush on Davida she was light skin and pretty. After that fight they had to give my sister her respect for not backing down. But this was nothing compared to what was to come, this was only getting her prepared. I remember a time we were in church for Sunday school, and this kid kept bothering my sister so I pulled out a blade and sliced him right there in the church. I was about 5 years old at that time and don't know what I was thinking. After that incident we were not allowed to come back.

CHAPTER TWO:

Summertime In SC

I was a little chubby kid with tight jeans and tight sweaters. I thought I was cool. My sister was tall and slim with high water jeans on, long feet, and huge glasses. We would see our older brother Darren maybe once a year in the summer when we'd visit South Carolina. I use to love those trips coming down on Grey Hound and other times we would ride with Jim Ford who made trips back and forth. My brother stayed with my aunt and uncle who raised him. My Uncle Shummer was a quiet man and my Aunt Mattie was the disciplinary. She didn't play, and we were afraid of her. Being in her house you had to go to church on Sunday, no ifs, ands, or buts. I caught a couple of beatings from her for wetting the bed. This small-framed older woman would beat you with the strength of two young men.

We would sit in the kitchen and watch TV a lot together, a little black and white with a hanger for an antenna. They had pigs in the yard: they had chickens, and they had dogs. All their dogs were friendly except for Pauline; she didn't seem to like us very much. But one of my uncle pigs got loose and was charging toward me and Tasha; I thank God that Pauline was there because she intercepted. She never seemed to like us but that particular day she had our backs and went after him.

I used to love riding with my aunt. She would go see different family members a lot and take us with her. I can still see her small frame today driving that big car with both hands. She would always be in the kitchen cooking us a full course meal. She'd go outside and grab a chicken and bring it back kicking and screaming. I saw her wring the neck a few times like she had no fear. She had a good system for getting children to eat their food. She sat your plate in front of you and your dessert, but you could not touch the dessert until you were done eating. Back then you couldn't tell an adult what you did and didn't want to eat; you'd get popped real fast. Everything they cooked was going on your plate. I always felt like that chicken from the outside didn't taste as good. It just had another type of taste. Maybe because I watched it being murdered, I don't know. I would eat all that country food on my plate just to get to that cake. Darren would always kick Tasha up under the table to let her know he wanted her cake.

She would be scared and give him the cake. I was a little fella sitting at the table watching this but my aunt and uncle never caught it. He knew not to try that with me because I was greedy, and I was going to eat my cake. Plus he knew I would tell on him, I didn't play that cause I only ate the food to get the cake. My aunt and uncle actually raised my mother, her sister, and two brothers. They were all born in South Carolina and moved to New York when they got in their 20s. My brother was the last child they raised, they never had children of their own so they loved for us to come down and spend the summer. When I'd wake up in the morning wet, I knew my beating was coming. I couldn't cover it up because she had access to the covers and sheets. It's funny when I think about it now, that I got beatings for something I did when I was asleep.

Whenever we would be in South Carolina, my mother would come later. To see her enter a room always put joy in my heart, I loved to see her coming. As much as I would enjoy our stay I think I enjoyed the trips back even better. I loved riding all those hours and just look out the window and see trees and be deep in thought. Even now, whenever I'm riding my mind is somewhere else.

CHAPTER THREE

Public School 25

We went to PS. 25 on Lafayette and Throop in Bed Stuy where we moved to. We lived on Throop, between Lexington and Green. Tasha and I would walk home together and sometimes other people we knew. I had a crush on this girl in the first grade, her name was Kimberly McKnight. She was light skinned with long hair and pretty eyes. I was way too shy to make a move on her. She asked me one day did I have a girlfriend, and I acted like I did, not realizing that might have been my opportunity. My homeboy Jaimy from around the corner liked her too, but neither one of us had enough heart.

I remember being upset with Jaimy when he and Kimberly had on the same Nikes. In my mind that meant that he had a way better shot at her than me. So I went home and asked my mother to buy me some Nikes, she didn't know what in the world I was talking about. Darren was staying in New York with us at the time, so he drew a pair of Nikes on a paper to show my mother. After that I got my Nikes, but I never did get the girl. PS. 25 was cool, they had this thing called "Funny Hat Day." It was a little competition for the whole school. We would take a hat and put all kind of stuff on the hat so we could win. We never did, but it was fun. I was in the 1st and Tasha was in the 3rd grade, making enemies fast. A lot of the kids in her class, mainly guys, didn't like her cause of her big glasses. Every day the guys would pick on her in class. I'm over here trying to live a peaceful life, and she was over there making enemies. Tasha would be fighting guys in school and out of school. I would enjoy my whole day at school up until 3:00pm because I knew what was coming.

At 3:00pm every day came some drama, and I would be caught in the middle of it. I would be scared because the 3rd graders were taller than me so I wouldn't fight them back. And everybody that hated her also hated me when they found out I was her brother. I would stand there and watch her fight, just standing there crying. If there was any time at all to pull a blade out and start slicing, it was now. Tasha was handling those guys, she would not back down. Eventually I started getting little threats because of her. There was times when those guys wouldn't be coming after Tasha, they wanted me. I was scared to death; my sister had way more heart than I did. She even said to me one day, "How come you'll fight me but won't fight them back?" that was a very good question but I didn't have an answer. One day this guy name Shawn from her class and a few other guys wanted to use me as bait to get at another 3rd grader since they knew he hated me, but I felt the whole thing was a setup so I said NO!

The whole thing just smelled fishy to me and I wasn't walking into a trap. We got picked on a lot because of my sister's glasses. But everything came to a stop one day when our brother came to pick us up. Nobody knew we had an older brother, but when they found out, we had peace for a while. While we would be at school and my mother was at work, our house would get robbed. It was a three story building, and we had the first and second floor. Our neighbor upstairs had two teenage sons, who would help themselves to our VCR's and other items. My mother always knew it was them but to keep the peace she didn't do anything. Plus she was friends with their mother, so we'd replace the items so they could rob us again. We lived on a small block full of nosey people, a random person could have never robbed us, and got away with it, it was an inside job. The neighbor upstairs also had a daughter my age, and one day me and her had a fight, she beat me like I stole something. Up until this point I had never fought anyone but Tasha, so I wasn't a fighter.

She beat me well enough for me to never mess with her again. Back then I use to love to watch Hot Tracks, a music video show. I immediately fell in love with a group called New Edition; they had a song called Candy Girl. I thought they were the coolest group ever. They reminded me of a younger and cooler version of The Jackson Five. As time went on, they came out with a song called Cool It Now. I wouldn't take my eyes off the screen when that video came on. Meanwhile in school, the goons my age started noticing me and I became cool with this kid named Shateek (who later appeared on one of those court shows). Shateek was at least a year or two older than me and a good fighter. For some reason he took a liking to me.

One day some goons tried to assault me and I ran and got him, he came back by himself and told them I was off limits, and that was that. I respected the power and the props he had in the school. I also became cool with this guy name Frankie; he was short but nice with his hands. He wouldn't allow anyone to mess with me either. But just like Shateek he was older than me too, which meant when they graduated I'd be all alone, and I was. This guy name Gerod started extorting me, he told me I had to pay him for protection, or he was going to beat me up. I never ever told anyone, I was embarrassed to be paying for protection. I gave Gerod 50cents every day, not only to keep the wolves off me, but to keep himself off me as well. He spotted me on the weekend one time and still expected money from me, so I paid him. He was a year older than me, so that meant he wouldn't be around much longer either.

It's not easy going to school and focusing on your school work when you have to worry about bullies. I was friends with this white boy named Joey, he was cool, and everyone loved him from the students to the teachers. He was a very smart student and had a bright future ahead of him. One day he didn't come to school, we figured he was sick or something because he wasn't the type to play hooky. But the next day we found out that Joey did play hooky, and that he played on the train tracks and was crushed by a train. That was the first friend I ever had that died. This kid at school kept bothering me so I eventually fought him back. We got it on right in the hall one day and everybody gathered around to watch. He got the best of me in that fight and made my nose bleed. When it was over this teacher said to me, "You should have beaten his behind." She should have been telling me we were wrong. In my mind I did alright in the fight, but by her saying that it let me know I didn't do half as well as I thought I did. I was giving him all I had, but it wasn't good enough. But at least he knew I would fight him back.

That summer I remember the Jamaicans across the street brought their turntables outside and was blasting Doug E. Fresh and Slick Rick. They were jamming, and I was in a zone, I became a real hip hop head. My mother was nice to me and gave me a dog, I don't remember if it was given to us or she bought it. We would keep him in the back yard tied up. I would bring him out front sometimes to walk him and he'd run away. This happened at least 3 or 4 times before we decided to just let him go. Every single time that dog ran off he would head towards Quincy and Throop. It didn't occur to me at the time but that had to be the block where he came from. My brother use to hang with Kid. He was bad, nobody played with him. He was a long-haired, dry jerry curl thug. Kid would fight, but his whole thing was shooting. He shot his girlfriend's windows out one night because she wouldn't open the door. He would beat his women in the street and didn't care who was around to see it.

He used to fight his girlfriend Judy. She was beautiful, and I didn't understand what she saw in him. Some women just like bad guys because the good ones are boring. Judy had brothers and cousins, and none of them would say a word to Kid. It seemed like all the fly guys that I looked up to in 80's were all crack heads in the 90's. I liked how they dress, the women they had, their cars, everything. They were neighborhood celebrities in their own right. You know the guy that came around and all eyes was on him, and all the beautiful women you planned on dating when you got older, they was all fiends and strung out. The women didn't even look the same as they did when I was a child. Judy was one of them, I just knew when I got older I was going to have her. She was the baddest thing in Bed Stuy, a Top Model before there were Top Models. She was like Diana Ross in the hood, but later on she was hooked on that stuff. Beauty and crack don't mix; if one stay the other is going to go eventually. There was this older guy named John that use to stand on the corner by the tire shop that use to bother me and Tasha. One day we saw him on the corner and told Darren, he went down there to see what was up and John was mute.

Times began to get rough for us very quickly. Somehow my mother fell behind on the rent and the landlord was tired of waiting, so he put all our stuff out on the street. Tasha and I were being watched by a neighbor but my mother was still at work. As a child I was embarrassed so I can imagine how my mother felt when she came home to see all her furniture on the street. All the neighbors were outside, so it wasn't a secret, everybody knew. After this we left Brooklyn for a little while and went from Hotel to Hotel in Manhattan. We were homeless. Some Hotels we slept in were nice, but then there were others that were not so nice. My mother could have easily asked her mother for a place to stay but I guess pride wouldn't let her. The Telephone Company was on strike again, and we bounced around Manhattan for a few months. Even thinking about it now is kind of sad because you hate to see anyone in that situation, especially children, but God brought us through.

CHAPTER FOUR

Lexington Avenue

We moved in a one-bedroom basement apartment on Stuyvesant. This place was horrible. Three of us cramped up in one little tight space. We had one TV to watch and there were times when my mother wanted to watch Dallas and I wanted to watch the A-team. Our landlord lived on the top floor, and his son and his girlfriend Liz lived on the second floor. My mother and Liz became cool. Not friends, but cool. Liz seemed to be real nice but I guess that was to get close enough. While we were at school and my mother was at work, Liz and her man robbed our apartment, taking our one TV and VCR, and other items. We immediately knew who did it. One morning our mother was walking us to school and my mother stepped to Liz, I guess she got smart or something because my mother started hooking off on Liz, and Tasha jumped in.

While they were beating on Liz, I picked up a trash can lid and threw it at Liz, but I never threw any punches because I kept thinking her man would come. After that we moved to Lexington Avenue, between Throop and Sumner. We had a three-bedroom apartment on the 2nd floor, and we felt like we were moving on up. Jam Master Jay's sister lived on the 3rd floor, I was cool with her husband but I didn't like her. Our next door neighbor was Ms. Corrine, she used to drink real heavy then pee in the hallway. She had a grandson that used to stay with her from time to time named Robert. They called him Pop cause he was cool, and him and my sister started talking. He also had a brother by the name of Willy who I really became cool with; he would be back and forth from Bed Stuy, Brownsville, and Harlem. I started hanging with this dude on the block named Mark. I didn't really care for him at first cause he was a Catholic school kid, the nerdy type. Terrell lived across the street, I knew him from around the corner. I also knew Lamean, Jared, and Omar from around the corner as well, and they lived a few houses down. I started hanging with Mark when I found out he had a Nintendo and a bunch of games.

We really didn't have too much in common he was kind of arrogant. But the more I went over his house to play games I saw past all of that and realized he was cool. I also started hanging with Goo from Gates Avenue, and he and I were tight for a hot minute. We use to go to the park jams in the early 80's and watch Shorty Gold and Microphone freestyle at block parties. I used to look on and wanted that kind of attention. I especially liked the way they had the girl's attention. Goo would come and hang on Lexington with me sometimes, but we mostly hung out on Throop Avenue with Shorty Gold, Steve-O, and some more people. One day my sister and I was riding our bikes down Quincy street, and Slop and his brother Forty started chasing us, so we dipped through the back of the projects to come out on the Gates side. My sister was ahead of me and we were getting away, but as soon as I hit the Gates side I ran smack dead into a pregnant woman who had to be about 8 or 9 months pregnant.

I felt horrible; I kept telling her I was sorry. Another reason I felt so bad because the pregnant girl on the ground was Goo's sister. I knew her, but she didn't know me. I wanted to be able to tell my side before anyone else could. So I saw Goo and Steve-O on Throop and I told them what happened how I was being chased, Goo ain't say nothing, but Steve-O said if that baby dies, I'm dead. Goo and I still hung out after that for a little while, and the baby lived. I started hanging out with Kev from Quincy and Tompkins. He was cool; he knew everybody and their momma. We would stand on the corner of Quincy and Tompkins and everybody that passed by, guy or girl, he knew them. He took me in his house one day where I noticed there was no evidence of an adult living there, and we were just kids. He had guns in his crib, bulletproof vest hanging in the closet, like he was ready for war. One day he came by my house and left a loaded 357 and said he'd be back later. When he came back later, he wanted me to come with him and about 6 other kids to do some robberies, so I went.

We walked around Bed Stuy looking for victims. It was the first time I carried a gun. We walked around for maybe a little over a half an hour and didn't see anybody we could get. Deep down something kept telling me to give them the gun and go home. I ignored that voice on the inside of me for a while because I didn't want to seem like a punk, like I was scared or something. The devil is good at getting young black males to do crimes in the ghetto by asking one question: "You scared to go jail?" The more I tried to ignore that voice, I just felt like I should take my behind back home. One kid in the crew didn't have a gun, so I handed him the one I had and said I'm going home and I'd see them later. I went straight home and didn't think anything else of it that night. I found out later, that "something" that told me to go home was on point. After I went home, all of those dudes got locked up on weapon charges. I got away from them just in time, but later found out they thought I went home and called the police on them.

Setting them up was the furthest thing from my mind, but I guess they thought they were such good criminals somebody had to snitch on them. But when are you walking around with 5 or 6 other guys and your hands are in your coats, you look suspicious? One night while hanging with Lamean and his brother Jared, the Cadillac club pulled up on the block deep. It was about 10 cars and a bunch of people in all of them and they were all getting out. They were going next door to look for Rome. The way they jumped out the cars you knew it was beef. I always liked Rome; he was very well known and liked. That night I was scared for him because it was on. Any time you see goons going in the person's yard and the neighbor's yard, it's on. But Rome's brother answered the door and said he wasn't in there, that's what he told them but he was home. I never found out what Rome did, but he pissed off a whole club. I was getting $10 allowance every week, so I would walk downtown Brooklyn to the Wiz, maybe 30-40 blocks and buy a record for $9.99.

I didn't have any money left for the bus so I would walk back. I loaded up on records every week; Run-DMC, Joe Ski Love, Eric B & Rakim, Just-Ice, Audio Two, KRS-One, The Force MD's, and LL Cool J just to name a few. I was in love with Hip Hop when Just-Ice came out with "Latoya" that was the jam. But nothing could compete with "Eric B. for president". I was going to summer school at the time and there was this pretty light skin girl named Patricia. She lived in downtown Brooklyn. One day we were coming back from a school trip and she pointed out her projects, so I locked it in my memory. I walked all the way downtown to see her. I bumped into this guy from summer school named Shawn that I was cool with and told him where I was going. I also ran into the guy that Patricia was talking to, Jermaine, and me and him spoke briefly. I lied to him and told him that I lived down there. I was real shy at the time, but I just wanted to see Patricia. So I went to her building, and I saw a few people outside but I didn't see her.

Then all of a sudden her and another girl came out of the building. She asked me what I was doing around there and I told her I had an aunt that lived in that building. I lied and also made up a floor, but I was glad to see her. I took the elevator to the 10th floor and just stayed up there for a while before coming back down. I went through all this, not even to kick it with her but to look at her. We get back to summer school and her boyfriend Jermaine is telling Shawn that I live around there, and I overheard Shawn telling him no he doesn't, he went to see

Patricia. Now why my man going to tell the girl's boyfriend I went to see her? He never came to me for drama so he must have asked her and she told him my aunt live in her building. I went over there at least one more time to stalk her, and was walking home like 11:00pm that night, and happened to walk down my grandmother's block, her and my aunt was getting out of her car at the same time.

When I saw them I just knew I was in trouble. I was a little kid away from home that late. We made small talk, and I kept it moving. Some time passed, and I started going to PS 324 on Gates avenue. I was pretty much cool with everybody, my bullying days was over, and so I thought. I use to hang with Mya from Gates and Lewis, he knew everybody. Every day at 3:00pm a bunch of dudes would be waiting outside the school to flip on people. I was by the gym one day and said something to this pretty girl that she took the wrong way and she threatened me. She told me that she was going to get me jumped at 3:00, so instead of going out the back door with the whole school and get beat up, I dipped out the front door. One day after school we were coming out and Drew (from Gates) threw his book bag on the ground in front of some guys and dared them to step on it. And if they would have, Gates Avenue would have jumped on them. It was a rumor that Big Daddy Kane lived around the way on Lewis Ave., but I didn't believe it. You're telling me one of my favorite rappers live around here with us? So one day I was walking down Lewis with the Roosevelt crowd and saw Kane outside washing his white Volvo. So I yelled out "Yeah Kane" because he said that on "The Wrath of Kane". Why did I say that? They thought another dude said it and got on him bad. In the hood black people have this thing about jocking.

I didn't see Kane everyday, so I spoke. Why not, I was playing his music in the house? One night Jared and I were coming from Roosevelt projects and Kane white Volvo was parked in front of his building so we stopped. We were just standing there looking at his car and he came out of the building. Here I am standing in front of my favorite rapper and didn't know what to say but the "S" word. The only thing that would come to mind was, "You have a nice car", and Kane said thanks and got in and drove off. Kane had on all his jewels, a nice black leather jacket with Big Daddy Kane in white writing. He also had on a pair of Nikes that I never seen before or after that day, he was fly. When he left me and Jared said we should have asked him for a ride so people on the block could see us getting out. When we got back on the block nobody was outside so it wouldn't have mattered anyway, they would have thought we were lying. I was walking to school one morning, and I walked pass about 8 guys standing in front of the projects on Gates and Lewis, and they said Yo come here for a minute. Against my better judgment I turned back and went. They surrounded me and wanted my MCM jacket.

MCM was hot back then, I had the whole suit, but that day I just wore the jacket. One of them grabbed my jacket and asked what school I went to, I said 324, so he said he didn't want that kind of heat and handed the jacket back. But another kid grabbed it and said I'll take it and jetted upstairs in the building. A few weeks after that the same guy that said he didn't want that kind of heat, saw me walking to school another morning. He asked me could I go in the projects and knock on his girlfriend's door because her mother doesn't like him. I know what you're thinking and I'm thinking the same thing, now. I went in the building to help him out, and he immediately knocked me to the floor and pulled out a knife on me. I started saying something to him and he told me to shut up, and began to take my new sneakers off my feet, and left me his raggedy kicks. Instead of going to school I went back home, and my mother called detectives to come to the house.

I was down the street watching them at my house but I was scared to point out anybody, so we dropped everything. While in 324, I figured I'd go back and visit PS 25. When I came out the back of the building and let the door slam shut, I saw about 15 guys across the street coming toward me. I kept walking, and they surrounded me. "Yo where you from?" They said. I said I'm from Lexington. They said "you know Malik?" I said yeah. I only knew Malik because he was popular in 324, but we didn't know each other personally. When I said that, they assumed I was saying me and Malik was from the same block and left me alone, but he was from the next block. Nevertheless his name got me out of a bad situation that day, how much more will the name of Jesus?

Tasha was hanging with a bunch of girls from Greene and Throop, and I started liking one of them, a light skin girl named Donna. I know what you're thinking everybody, he liked was light skin. I liked Donna, Mark liked Tonya, and Willy and Trina had something I can't describe. We use to go on their block and hang with them a lot. Donna was the first girl that I had actually talked to in a long time. One day I threw a hooky party at the house and all the girls from that block came except Donna, so I went after Sherry. We kissed and stuff and I remember her telling me, "I'm telling Donna" hold up, you were kissing me back but you telling? She didn't lie either. When Donna got home from school she told. Donna and I only talked for like 2 weeks, so it wasn't really a relationship, but you couldn't tell me that. I used to tell Mark and Big Will (Willy) when you see Donna geek it (put in a good word). When I saw Trina, Tonya, or my sister I would say geek it. I had everybody and their mother trying to geek it for me and it didn't work. I eventually gave up after about 100 tries. You have to know when to hold them and know when to fold them.

I was on Greene Ave. with Mark and Terrell when this girl Cocoa was saying something slick out of her mouth, so I punched her in the face. She stumbled and went down the stairs and reached for a razor to slice me so I punched her in the face again. Then she threatened to get me jumped, so I punched her in the face again. She made some threats and left to go get the dudes from Gates Ave, I already knew some of them so I didn't move. It just happened they all went to Coney Island, so she went and came back with some other dudes. When I saw them coming down the block, I dipped in Mark house to lie low. She brought them straight to Mark door to ask for me. They told Mark to let me know they were looking for me. I hid that night, but I never hid another night and I saw the guys she brought back and nobody ever said anything. Me and the main guy she wanted to get me sat in Tompkins Park drinking and laughing about the situation. I asked him, how are you going to come see me for hitting a woman and you just got out of jail for beating your woman?

We thought that was funny. Eventually our Lexington avenue apartment started getting robbed as well.

They took numerous VCR's from us, but this time we weren't sure who did it. But one of our upstairs neighbors had a son who we believe came down the fire escape and went back up. If a criminal have enough guts to come in your house, rob you, and damage the place, they're not going to lock your door back. Our doors were still locked which means the fire escape was used. After a while I didn't like Lexington that much, our building was right next to a huge lot. We had mice really bad in that place. You wouldn't see or hear them in the daytime, but at night, they all played freeze tag and red light, green light, 123. I used to hate trying to go to sleep there because you could feel them climbing up on the cover at night. And mice have such a disgusting odor to them. They would get in the dresser and bite on the clothes and get in the cabinet into the cereal. One night I woke up and looked in the kitchen and going in the trash can was a huge rat, not a mouse, but a rat, I was terrified.

New York rats are very healthy; they eat better than us. We had serious hard times and no help at all from my father. He would come around once a year and we had to get use to him all over again. One time Tasha and I was playing cards with him and kept referring to our father as "him" and he said something to us about it. But it was weird to call a man daddy that we barely knew. Tasha worshipped the ground he walked on and he couldn't do any wrong in her sight. I held it all against him because I wanted and needed a father and I didn't have one. A woman can't teach a boy how to be a man, he needs a father for that. My mother wouldn't even ask him for anything. If we didn't have it, we just didn't have it. Plenty of days we were in the dark because our lights got cut off and my mother would light candles. She always used to tell us, "It's not going to always be like this!" and that was a little comforting to us. We would go a couple of months and they would be back off again. My friends would ask me can I have company and I had to make up a lie because we were in the dark. Big Will, Mark, Tasha, and I were hanging in front of the building one night just having a good time.

Big Will was a very funny guy; he would have your stomach hurting. One night he was ranking on Trina, and he talked about her for like an hour straight nonstop. Trina wasn't there, and she was my sister friend, but even Tasha had to laugh. Big Will was hilarious; I believe he would have made a great comedian. Mark was funny too but nobody could hang with Big Will. This Jamaican gave me some weed to sell, a bunch of nickel bags. I didn't smoke at that time but I gave Big Will a bag. I kept the whole stash he gave me and didn't pay him anything. He looked for me for a while and would come by the house every day. Even till this day I believe someone talked him out of killing me. I never set out to keep his stuff, it just happened that way. I didn't know anything about selling drugs and didn't know who to sell it to either. Most of the people I knew were drinkers, not smokers.

Years earlier my father gave me some of his Budweiser beer and I drank it all. It sowed a seed in me because I enjoyed that rugged taste. Things like that may seem cute to some parents until it becomes a problem later. Like kids being grown and saying curse words, to some parents that's funny until those same kids are cursing them out later. One day I figured I would go and buy a beer, me, and Mark. I bought a St. Ides tall can, and I was nice off that one can. My father sowed that seed years earlier, and I remembered the taste and I wanted it. My mother use to have a little mini-bar in the house and I would hit it now and then. I wouldn't hit it hard and make it obvious but I was working on it. I became a 15-year-old alcoholic.

Mark started distancing himself, hanging with his cousin Matt in Marcy Projects. They put Mark on to Calvin Klein, then I started going with Mark to Tom, Dick, & Harry's getting them too for $40. I had a new girlfriend named Tiffany, she had brown skin. I would go hang out at her home and she would come to mine. One day me, her, and Mark was sitting together talking, and we were talking about her but she never knew. Mark and I hung around one another so long that we had code language. We were sitting there calling her a liar and she never knew. We didn't say anything about her looks because she was on point. The same guy that my brother stepped to on the corner years before liked Tiffany and hated me because I had her. I spotted her one day walking and talking to him and his boys, so I was done. This guy hates my guts and you're his friend? So we broke up. My sister became friends with Herman, Slop and Forty brother, the two guys who caused me to run into the pregnant girl. Herm was a little older than me but we became cool. He and I both had a love for Eric B. & Rakim's music.

I started drinking more when I started hanging with him. My boy Trop started dating Herm cousin Toya, I use to like her, but he got to her first. I was known for rapping and was nice with mine too. There was a studio down the street from Herm he used to go to. He did a little DJ'ing and had a female rapper. They took me to the Roxy with them one day. We passed Too Short on the street and I spoke to him. I was kind of shocked to see him walking the streets of Manhattan and to be by himself like he wasn't scared. At the Roxy Kool G. Rap was supposed to perform but for some reason he got mad and left. King Sun was there, Fat Joe, Cypress Hill, Large Professor, and Das Efx, this was my first show. Das Efx performed "They Want Effects" and Large Professor performed his banger, "Faking the Funk". Hanging around Herm I became cool with the dudes off the next Lexington and Quincy. I was supposed to be one of the artist they promoted at the studio, and Mark was my DJ. While we were all riding together in a van one day they asked me to kick a rhyme, so I joked with them and said my freestyles ain't free. They took offence to that and kicked me out of the studio. One night we were all at Supreme crib and two guys from the projects on Quincy was there and wanted to battle me. One of them was down with Gang Starr and was in the "Just to Get a Rep" video.

And was also on the back of an album that Mark happened to have with him. We recorded it and Supreme was on the turntables, and I slayed both of them with one verse. I ran into Jeru the Damaja on the train and I said, "I took out y'all boy Jermaine." He said, "That's my cousin." Jeru was busy trying to holla at some girl on the train that wasn't paying him any mind. Either she didn't know who he was, or she knew and didn't want a rapper who was riding the train. I ran into Master Ace one day in

Brooklyn, I spoke to him, but he didn't want to leave his man out so he let me know he had Craig G. riding with him, so I spoke to him too but I wasn't a fan. His verse was the only verse on "The Symphony" that nobody liked. Me, Mark, and his cousin Matt was at the Chinese restaurant on Tompkins, I already ordered and stood outside catching some air. This guy walked up to me and showed me his gun on his waist and said, tell your boys to get up out of there. I told them yo let's go this dude is about to rob the place and I didn't have to tell them twice, we were gone. I started hanging out a lot with Trop's cousin, Ceasar. He would come around a lot and we kicked it. What made us bond is that he would drink like me. Me, Mark, and Big Will was together one night when Mark's cousin Matt came through with Marcy projects.

So they walked down to the next Lexington, and me and Will walked with them. While we were standing there, Black, his cousin Low, and two more of their boys walked up. The Marcy project dudes was about 12 deep, but they all got shut down by Black, Low, and two other dudes. The only one that opened their mouth from Marcy was Matt, those other guys didn't say a thing. I also became cool with Divine, Star, Shawn Boogie, and they whole Rebel Cartel. One night me and Ceasar was walking down Fulton St. and saw a whole Brady bunch of dudes in front of McDonald's so Ceasar said let's cross the street, I said no. In Brooklyn dudes don't have a problem crossing the street to come after you. The closer we got I realized it was the Rebels, like 60 strong. We kicked it with them for a minute and went our way. One night, Mark and Peter went to Greene avenue store, and some dude asked Peter what he was looking at and shot him in the face. Peter was still alive but his face was swollen for a long time. Mark ran to my house to get me to come out there, but I was like nah.

I wasn't the type to just stand over people and watch a tragedy. When people would get hit by cars in the hood I wouldn't stand in the crowd, how is that going to help them? Peter was Jamaican and his family didn't play they went around the neighborhood looking for the guys that night. Lexington Ave. was fun, but my mother found a better spot.

CHAPTER FIVE

Fulton Street

I started going to Boys N Girls High school and had to battle every single day. One dude in there found out I could rap and he brought somebody to me every day. It seemed like he knew all the rappers in the school. I was slaying this kid in the locker room and the crowd was amazed, but that same day we all got detention. While sitting in detention I started rapping again and the dude next to me said "That's what got us in here in the first place" as if I told him to watch the battle. On my way to the gym one day I spotted some money on the floor. I looked around for a minute because this was too easy. I bent down and scooped it up, and right after I got it the door of the gym opened, that was close. I went and bought me some sneakers with it. I told my mother and she accused me of selling drugs. I was hurt, she didn't believe me.

One night I was talking to my home girl from Smurf Village on the phone and her man got on the phone and got smart. By this time my heart was getting bigger. I said to Mark "let's go over there",, and Mark said whatever. I also asked Black, but Black said nah, he didn't like coming off the block at all. Me and Mark went down there and knocked on her door, she claimed her man left but I believe he was in the house hiding. My mother moved us on Fulton Street in the projects across from Boys N Girls high school. It was a nice 3-bedroom apartment. My man Mark would visit and Big Will would come through too. The last time Big Will came to the crib he told Tasha she could sing, he really pumped her up. After that I didn't see Big Will for a long time. Mark had seen him and said he wasn't doing that great, and how he gave him some clothes to get on his feet.

I went back on Lexington one day to hang with Black; he was standing on the corner beefing with this Jamaican cat named Debo. Out of nowhere Black smacked Debo, and Debo pulled out on Black in broad daylight. Black dipped to his family house around the corner, and came back with all of them, but Debo was gone. Black's family wasn't a stranger to beef, and they stuck together. One night Fat Boy called me and said the whole crew was at his house and for me to come over. He lived on Fulton too so I walked down there, I wanted a drink or two. Fat Boy opened the door and there was nobody there, none of the crew. His mother was in her bedroom lying down and he was in the living room watching a porno. Fat Boy loved to play with guns, so I thought this dude was about to try something. Soon as I walked in I saw a big floor model TV playing pornography. I came in and he closed the door behind me, I never sat down.

I made up some excuse and got up out of there. It was already rumored that he played crazy to escape from doing some serious jail time, but I don't think he was playing, he was crazy. Me and Mark wasn't really hanging tight at this point, he was spending a lot of time in Marcy.

We were talking about Big Will one day and about going to see him. It's been awhile since Big Will came to Bed Stuy, since he was staying in Howard in Brownsville. We decided we were going to pay him a surprise visit since that was our boy. We both decided on next week and agreed. When next week came, I said to Mark let's go another time, but for some reason I just wasn't feeling it. We both agreed to go see him another time. I was hanging on the corner of Throop and Lexington when Douglas came over to tell me Big Will was murdered. My heart dropped I couldn't believe it; he told me Will's best friend killed him. Will's cousin was dating the best friend, he shot her first and Will jumped in, then he shot Will too. He ran out the apartment and Big Will ran behind him, falling to his death. Losing Will was a major loss; he was more than a friend. He was a brother. Mark, Tasha, and I went to the wake. We saw his cousin outside who got shot too; I really didn't want to speak to her because I felt like it was her fault Will was dead. But I gave her hug anyway, it was hard.

I blamed her because in my mind she had no business dating Will's best friend Shawn, because she used to date Shawn's brother. We spoke to his brother Robert aka Hype outside as well. Tasha and Mark went in to see the body while I stalled outside talking to Hype. I eventually made my way in to see Big

Will, and it was hard seeing him like that lying there stiff, not really looking like himself. But we paid our respects and said our goodbyes. I realized the same night that Big Will was murdered was the night that me and Mark was supposed to go see him. That year Nas came out with Illmatic and changed the game. Nas had the rap game in a choke hold for real. I use to record Stretch Armstrong and Bobbito show. Nas would go up there and freestyle. All of a sudden in 1994 I got tired of my life and wanted a change. I gave my life to the Lord and started going to church. I was telling everyone I knew about Jesus. I gave Mark all my Hip Hop cassette tapes, and that was big, believe me. All I wanted to listen to was gospel. I felt like a brand new person but in the same body.

I started going to Bible Study and had Mark going with me. I even took my boy Troy too, he had to have a drink before he went but I was glad he was going. I would just dig in the word of God all day long when I was home. A lot of things I didn't really understand, and didn't have anybody to make it plain for me. It's important that every new convert have a mentor; not a buddy, not a friend, but a mentor. I would go around the way and try to witness to my homeboys on the corner. I wanted them to have this new life that I found. Some of them would listen but it was going in one ear and out the other. I used to try to win my sister too, she said to me one day, "I feel like you my big brother!" The church I was going to was dead; I didn't see any kind of move of the spirit. I never saw anyone get saved or delivered there. I kept going around the guys talking about Jesus and the end of the world. I had zeal for God but not according to knowledge. My problem was I thought I could live a new life hanging around my old friends, but I was wrong. I remember standing there with them while they were drinking and all of a sudden I wanted a drink. Here I am a Christian on the corner with thugs, and now I want a beer.

Later that night I went and bought me a 40oz of St. Ides and hid from everybody. I was ashamed and trying to hide because of the embarrassment. Everybody knew I gave my life to the Lord, so I didn't want to be judged. A mentor would have come in good right here if I just had one person to tell me I could get back up. All I had was the dudes in the street and that's why I spent so much time around them. If some brothers from the church had taken me under their wing, I could have held on. But, it was my fault and my relationship with God that I threw away. I only walked with God for 4 months, I stopped going to church, and nobody looked for me. I was back in the world. Me, Black, Derrick, and a few other people put our heads together to do a robbery. His cousin Mike wanted us to come to his job and wait in the wings for the person that handles the checks after they come from the bank. We rolled over there about 6 deep and everybody got in place. We had some on this corner and some on another corner, everybody was in position. We saw the guy who had the checks make his way to the bank as we watched in the cut. We had our getaway driver so we could make it out of there with no problem.

I went from going to church and telling people about Jesus to being a part of a jooks. I fell from grace, and now I'm worse than before. Bibles, Churches, Prayers and Parables were the furthest thing from my mind, I wanted that money. The area we were in had a little bit of traffic as far as people walking back and forth. We looked on as the guy made his way back from the bank with all the employees' money in a bag. Something somewhere went wrong, and we weren't able to get our man. Some people didn't follow the plan we had mapped out. We came out here for nothing. I use to hang out at the corner store of Throop and Lexington a lot Poppy loved me. I would get free beer and free lucies all the time. Sometimes I even got free heroes. The cops came and locked up Poppy for running numbers in the back of the store and that left one man in the store alone.

Instead of holding him down I became a part of what was about to go down. My whole block rushed the store, guys and girls; we went up in there and took everything we wanted, from food, to drinks, to cigarettes. Imagine a whole block in one store scattered like roaches. I never stopped to think I was wrong and all the times Poppy looked out for me and showed me love. After we robbed the place, we all went back on the block and laughed. A few days later when Poppy got out he was brokenhearted, he couldn't believe that I would rob his store after all he's done for me. His worker told him I was involved and it hurt Poppy. I couldn't lie and say I wasn't there, because he already knew. I could see the pain in his eyes; when he spoke he held back tears. I was wrong. Shortly after that Poppy left the hood and we got a brand new Poppy. I worked my way into favor with this Poppy as well. My name was so good in his store that if someone went in there and said Tron is going to pay for it, they gave them their stuff. I built a relationship with the new owner.

CHAPTER SIX:
South Carolina Vacation

Me and my cousin Justin from Howard projects in Brownsville were on our way down south for the summer. Our grandmother had relocated to Blenheim SC, from Brooklyn. My brother was already living back in South Carolina again. We got down there in the woods and partied like rock stars. My brother would come by and pick me up with his crew and we'd go and hit a hole in the wall, most of the time just to play pool and pick up women. I was a young man, but I wanted to show my brother and his boys that I could hang with the best of them. My brother's best friend name was Jimmy; he was a crook that couldn't be trusted, but I liked him. Jimmy was always trying to get over on somebody; he always had some kind of scheme lined up. My brother was dating this older Caucasian female named Linda, and they were complete opposites. Her and my brother used to dress alike as if they were still locked in the 80s.

Linda seemed real cool and sweet when we met. I use to love hanging with my brother I looked up to him. We were just riding and drinking all day hitting hole in the wall after hole in the wall. One day a few of us stopped on this dirt road where some girls were and got out. Everybody was in the road talking and having fun. We looked up and here came Linda driving like a maniac towards us. I can't even lie to you; my brother was scared for his life. She came and had her gun on her lap and her hair looked real wild. I believe somebody tipped her off, like one of his boys. He jumped in the car with her and left me behind to find my own way back. Justin was just a little younger than me so we would leave him at the house with Nana (grandma). He was cool he just wasn't ready to stomp with the big dogs yet so we left him on the porch. When I was in the house, I would listen to South Carolina's corny radio stations. It wasn't nothing like the Hot 97 and WBLS that I was used to. My brother and Linda would come and get me and Justin sometimes to take us riding.

It seemed like the only thing worth doing in South Carolina was ride. On Sundays everyone would head over to the Blue Light down in the country. It would be a large crowd out there, guys, and girls. Being Darren's brother and being from New York made me an instant celebrity with the country girls. I use to roll with Jimmy, Merick, Clyde, Darren, and some others. Every night they brought me back to the house drunk. I counted out the exact change one day for some ice cream and took it to the store in Blenheim. I put the ice cream on the counter along with my change and the guy at the register counted it and said it wasn't enough, so I took his word for it and went back to the house. The next day I happened to count the change again, and saw that it was the correct change. Me, Darren, Jimmy, Justin, and Linda went to the store, and I said to the guy in the store "I handed you the correct change yesterday, you can't count?" He said something slick out of his mouth and I punched him in the face. Another guy was sitting to the side and they pulled out guns on me. The thing that saved me was some guys pulled up for some gas. Had it been night time and nobody around when I did that, I would have been buried in the woods somewhere.

One day my grandmother argued with me for no reason at all, telling me how my mother doesn't love me. I was always under the impression that my grandmother didn't like my mother and that she favored her oldest daughter, my Aunt Lucille, who bought the double wide Nana stayed in. She argued with me and I said a few words back, nothing disrespectful, but I should have shut my mouth. Justin found Nana dead in the living room the next day, slumped over. I was in so much shock that I didn't even call the cops. I went next door to my cousin Debra house, and she came back to the house with me and made the call. Before my grandmother passed she already told my Aunt Lucille that we had a disagreement, and somehow it went around the family that I killed her. She mostly was talking by herself, but they said I killed her. While I was across the road getting my cousin Debra, my cousin was stealing money from Nana's purse. Our grandmother lying on the floor dead, and he had his hands in her purse. He gave me some money so he wouldn't go down alone. He handed me $50 that I took and put in my pocket but never spent it.

He went and bought a sweat suit with his half of the money; all this was before the funeral. My mother, Lucille, and my Uncle Tyson all came down. Not only did Nana tell Aunt Lucille we were arguing, she also told her how much money she had. Aunt Lucille asked me for the money and I gave her the $50 I had and asked Justin for that purple looking clown suit he bought. Me and Darren were getting on him because he bought a sweat suit from the women's section. I don't know what part of Brownsville they did that in. Didn't matter how much we got on him. That little dude thought he was cool. I believe deep down I had a conscience because I hesitated on spending that money. I had several chances to spend it. I was there when he bought the clown suit, and I could have got one too. My Uncle Tyson (Justin's father) asked me why was me and Nana arguing, I told him that she was telling me my mother didn't love me. I could tell that he felt like I killed her too. My mother never asked me about the argument but she knew. When family members came over for the setting up some of them was very cold towards me. I didn't even argue with her I just responded to one of her comments, but here I was an outcast in the family. I even had cousins who was telling people, "Don't mess with that boy, he killed his own grandmother." I didn't want my grandmother to die, I just wanted her to respect my mother and love her the same way she loved my Aunt Lucille. I didn't even go to her funeral, and to this day I don't regret it, because I didn't need everyone's attention on me like I'm the reason she was in the casket. I felt like with me not being there everyone was able to focus on saying goodbye to Alice Moses.

CHAPTER SEVEN

Back On L.E.X. Again

Now that I walked away from God I was hitting the bottle worse than before. I believe I had more to drink than a fish. I really started hanging with Troy then because we both loved beer. Everybody knew us, so when people would come to the store they would automatically say to one or both of us "you want a beer?" We moved back to Lexington, but on the next block, Lexington between Throop and Tompkins. Tasha lived around the corner on Greene Avenue. I was glad we were closer because I was getting tired of walking that far. I started talking to this girl Iesha whose mother lived on the next block, Lexington between Tompkins and Marcy. Me and Troy was at the twin's house, Darlene and Charlene, and Iesha was in their kitchen cooking.

She saw me and told one of them to tell me something. We were on our way to bible study but I told her I would be back.

I came back through and we kicked for a while. She was slim, brown skin and looked like a model; in fact she said she did model. We didn't really spend too much time on the phone because we saw each other every day. I must admit I caught feelings pretty fast. She had two kids a little boy and a girl. I use to go and pick the kids up from daycare, she put my name on the list to get them. One day while I had her son at the house. I started cooking and went outside and the door locked behind me. I was scared to death. I was ringing and ringing the bell for her son to answer the door but he was sleeping too hard. I just knew I was going to jail for killing her son. I had food on the stove and the boy in the house alone with my key upstairs. I went and told Black, and he let me up on the roof through the crack house. We crossed a couple of buildings and then I got down in my house, which was close. Iesha and I were good for a minute until she started saying if I didn't get a job she was leaving me.

My mother overheard that and she liked it. But it didn't last long, my mother couldn't stand Iesha. One day Iesha bought a bunch of groceries for our house and then she left. My mother came home and took everything she bought back out of the cabinets. I felt that was mean. Iesha came back by and asked me why the stuff wasn't in the cabinets and I made up some lie, but she knew better. Around this time, she started telling me she was pregnant and I was happy. I was telling everyone I had a baby on the way, then we broke up and she disappeared for a while. My mother kept saying to me "Tron get a job," but I didn't want a job. I just wanted to hang out and drink. So one morning when I came home from hanging out all night, I saw a long moving truck outside. She wasn't kicking me out; she was moving out and leaving me. What really hurt was, she said to me, "Tron you can at least help" I thought she was crazy. I'm about to be homeless and you asking me to help you move? I didn't help anybody. I stayed in that apartment a few more weeks with just my bedroom in it and had no idea how I was going to eat.

These Jamaicans asked me to sell some weed for them and I said yeah. They took me to the spot. It was an apartment where kids would come after school and buy weed like crazy. They had the weed stashed in the ceiling of the apartment. I messed around and rolled up a blunt and got paranoid. Whenever I looked out the window and saw somebody white come in the building, I got scared. The spot they had was a goldmine, high school kids was coming left and right, and I would slide it through the door. Even though it was a goldmine, I knew I couldn't keep working there. So I took some money for my time, in other words I paid myself for my time and trouble and got up out of there. The Jamaicans was highly upset with me because I left and because I paid myself. But that same spot got busted the week before and I couldn't take any chances. I didn't keep all the money; I paid me and left. Me, Stacy, Caesar, Terrell, and some more people walked around playing the knock out game.

This was the first time I had ever heard of it. Whoever you punched had to fall down but you couldn't pick your own victim; they had to be picked for you. We walked around for a good hour laying innocent people down. We didn't lay a hand on women, only men. The guy they picked for me I waited until I got all the way up on him and leaned into him real good and he went down. One guy we punched wouldn't go down, so we all started jumping him. We saw about 7 guys across the street that we didn't know, they came over and jumped on the guy with us. I never heard of that in my life, strangers helping you double team and outnumber somebody. Only in Brooklyn. I was running with Ceasar a lot at that time. My mother would give me money to go look for a job and we would drink the money. Then I'd tell her we looked for jobs in Manhattan. In those days we went to the honeycomb hideout, an apartment his mother had in Brownsville projects that she wasn't using.

You could also find us in Sheepshead Bay almost every other weekend. We were on the train headed to Manhattan when Ceasar tried to talk to this pretty light skinned girl and she sat there and ignored him. I was feeling nice off the beer so I stood up on the train and preached about how we should love one another and not see ourselves as more than other people. I even told them to turn to their neighbor and repeat after me, and they did it. I was shocked. I had the whole train's attention and New Yorkers are not the nicest or friendliest people in the world. After that Ceasar and I laughed about it for a while. I preached my initial sermon on a train to Manhattan. We were always doing and getting into something crazy. I came out one night on the block and nobody was out so I stood on the corner drinking. Some people came by that I knew from Quincy Street, but I didn't really mess with them.

I saw Divine and Ceasar, and the kids from Quincy asked us to walk with them somewhere. So I walked with them, that night it was a bunch of snow on the ground. I had on my brand new Fila boots, black and brown. A few of them went upstairs while the rest of us stayed downstairs. When they came back down and we started walking, we saw a bunch of dudes coming from out of nowhere running towards us. We were taking off because we were outnumbered. Everybody was getting away but for some reason I turned back because one of the kids was caught. I wanted to leave him. After all, he wasn't my man, and I just knew him. As much sense as it made to leave him I couldn't bring myself to do it, so I turned back to help. I was going hand to hand with one guy, and while I was fighting him I saw out the corner of my eye, the kid I went back to help took off running and leaving me. Next thing I know I'm fighting two guys, and the last thing I remembered I was surrounded by all of them and I tried to get off the ground and back on my feet, but I was knocked back down. Later, I found out that one of the guys that I was with went upstairs to curse out the grandmother.

I woke up to a camera flashing in my face inside 79th precinct. One of the guys that jumped me was sitting there with a female and was whispering threats to me not to tell. I didn't tell, not because his threats, but because I planned on getting him back. My head was huge, my lips, my face, everything was swollen. The police let me go, and I walked to the house and I remember being glad that nobody saw me outside. My mother came by the apartment the next day for something and came in and saw my whole head swollen and took me to the hospital. At Brooklyn-Jewish Hospital I was ashamed, everyone was looking at me like I was a monster. I left back out the hospital that night. My mother caught a cab and took me back to the apartment, when we hit the corner of my block she told the cab driver to wait while she ran in the store, she went in and grabbed me some oodles of noodles. While she was in there the cab driver turned around and said, "What in the world happened to you?" I didn't even feel like talking my lips was so big. I gave him the shortest version I could think of: I got jumped.

I stayed in the house a few days. Terrell came by the next day and had two girls with him, I peeped through the curtain, and there was no way I was opening that door for them. As time went on my man Troy would look out for me and feed me when he could and let me sleep on his floor when his grandparents went to sleep. I can't begin to tell you how much I appreciated that floor. I was officially homeless. One night I slept in the crack house in my tee shirt and it was freezing cold. I begin to plead with the Lord to get me out of that situation. Late one night I saw this dude that use to hang on our block so I crept up behind him and hit him. BOW!! He dropped to the ground and was lying there stiff, I took off running. The cops and the ambulance showed up, and the block was crowded but neither he nor anyone else knew who hit him. I stood in the crowd with everyone else; "I wonder what happened to him, is he alright?" After I got jumped, I didn't speak to Ceasar for a while because I felt like he left me for dead. But one day I went to his cousin's house and Ceasar was there about to leave.

Terrell said Ceasar was on his way to the Tempestt Bledsoe show, and he got two tickets, so I befriended him again for that extra ticket. We hopped on the train and headed to Manhattan to the show. Security didn't want to let me in at first because they smelled alcohol on me but I lied and said I only had a small can of Budweiser, but I really had a forty. I had already purposed in my heart that I would never go on a talk show without saying something on the mic. The show was guys vs. girls. They had the men sitting on one side and the women on the other side. I raised my hand and Tempestt came over giving me that Vanessa Huxtable smile. I wanted to make my presence known on the show so I decided to snap (rank, jank, and jones) on the people on the panel, and the whole audience was laughing. Ceasar tried to follow my lead and get his 5 seconds of fame too by raising his hand. When the show was over, I remember the whole audience walking down the stairs together, and the girls got me and Ceasar.

Talking about they're going to come to the show and they don't even have haircuts. I wasn't even mad; I laughed when she said it. The show came on a couple weeks later, and the day it came on everybody around the way saw it. After the show went off, I went to Tompkins Park and threw some shades on, that 5 seconds of fame went to my hand. I took some juice, one cup, and a bottle of gin to the park just so people could tell me they saw me. Like an hour later people were like I saw you on Tempestt show. My grandmother (my father's mother) even called to say she saw me on the show. Some days I was still struggling with how I was going to eat and my man Troy was still looking out for me. Black asked me if I wanted to sell crack, up until this point I never even considered selling crack, but now I just got tired of being hungry. The enemy will get you while you're at your lowest and offer you false hope that seems like help. I told him "yeah I'll do it" just so I could eat.

Clarence taught me the number one rule to the game: never sell to anyone you don't know. I started selling crack for Black, Debo, and Roy. Fiends was coming on the block all day long to get that stuff. Some crack heads surprised me, I saw some of the prettiest females Brooklyn had to offer asking for that white rock. I sold to business men in suits who were successful in life. This dude Shawn from my old block started slinging at the same time I did, he was an ex-crackhead. Shawn was clean now and he was fly. You could always tell when Shawn was back on that stuff again because he didn't care about his appearance and plus you'd see him carrying garbage bags on his back. I promise you Shawn was like an ant; he would have TVs, Couches, Beds, and all on his back walking down the street. It wasn't long before Shawn was smoking again; I was rooting for him because he tried to stay clean.

When we saw that garbage bag we didn't have to wonder what he was doing. This beautiful female cop came on my block one day dressed in plain clothes so I pushed up on her. We were standing there talking for a while then out of the corner of my eye I saw a crack head coming down the street toward me. This lady was moving extra fast and I was standing there thinking how I was going to play it. She walked right up to me and said I need something. I'm standing there with the lady cop, so I said I don't know what you're talking about and I gave her my back. The lady cop said to me go ahead, I know what you do. And I'm still trying to play it off, she had to convince me. Now, I'm thinking. Is this some kind of set up? The Police going to tell me to go ahead and make a sale? I did just want she told me to do and got that money.

One night we were all on the corner and Old Dirty Bastard from the Wu-Tang Clan stopped in front of us to let us know it was him in the car and nobody cared. His boy in the passenger seat thought it was hilarious and he was the only one. After that little unexpected interruption we got back to business, popping those bottles. While everyone else was putting their crack in obvious places like the mailbox where the police knew to look, I was putting my crack inside Walkmans. I'd take the cassette tape out and fill it with crack vials. One day the police approached me on the corner to check me and told me to lay my walk-man down. To make sure they didn't see the crack through the little window I laid it face down on the ground. Whenever the block saw the police check me, I would keep Debo and Roy work and just tell them the police took it. I took a nap in the crack house one day and overheard detectives outside the window, I peeped out, and these guys had battering rams about to knock the door down.

So I hid some crack underneath the mattress and went to the door and acted like a crack head. I was dressed nice, I had on jewelry, and was clean cut, but I played that crack head role better than Pookie. When I opened the door, they yanked me out, so I acted like I came to buy crack. They went in my wallet and saw the money and a few crack vials, they kept that but I didn't care. They yelled at me who else is in there? I said this drug dealer name Mike, please don't tell him I told y'all, he'll kill me. They said shut up and get the *BLANK* out of here; I took off and didn't come back till the next day. When I came back I went straight for the mattress where I hid the drugs, and it was still there. I walked down to DeKalb with Ceasar and Terrell one night to smoke some weed because we didn't want to smoke on the block.

We picked a building and sat there for a little while until it was all gone and came back. On the way back both of them was in front of me and all of a sudden I started walking into on-coming traffic. I wasn't even moving my legs; it was like I was inside someone else's body watching them walk. It was like something out of a horror movie. I looked down and my legs were moving fast toward the middle of the street. Traffic was getting closer ,so I yelled out to them to come and get me and they grabbed me just in time. Soon after I met this girl from Fort Green and she invited me to spend the night at her house so I went over there with her. I was a dog at the time and she wouldn't give me any so I waited till she went to sleep and I took off and left her door wide open. You have to understand that's not a good thing in Fort Green, especially at that time.

Ceasar and I headed out to Sheepshead Bay where his cousin Trop lived it was a party over there. We got there a little early Trop was in the back playing music kind of low. A few girls were in the kitchen and like 3 guys were in the living room. Since Trop had the music low, me and Ceasar could hear everything the 3 guys was saying about us. So I whispered to him to be ready, and he said he was ready. One guy came over to shake our hands and he shook Ceasar's hand first, then when he got to me I said "you don't get no love." I wasn't about to shake his hand and they over there talking about flipping on us. So he went back over in the corner to his crew. Then he came back again and said to Caesar, "oh you Trop cousin," then they shook hands again. He reached for my hand the second time and I said "Didn't I tell you, you don't get no love?" He snuffed me, and before his hand left my face my hand was on his face. He fell to the floor ,so I started stomping him out.

Then two other guys started swinging on me. Ceasar wasn't doing anything but standing there, and I realized I was alone. He claimed later he didn't see the two guys swinging on me... Right. So you're telling me while we're fighting and everyone else is looking at us you were watching the wall? I dipped through the kitchen and made it out of the party just in time. I got in the hall and had to dip through a sea of dudes. I heard some people chasing me but I didn't look back. I headed towards the bus stop. I got back in the hood and went straight to Star house on Gates and told them what happened. The next week me, Star, and Divine went back out there. Trop walked us around the projects to help us find the dudes. We saw a bunch of guys on a bench and went over there. We were outnumbered, but we came to war. None of those guys on the bench was there; I didn't recognize any of their faces. So we came back a week later this time it was more of us, I brought a team this time. We walked around again and couldn't find the dudes, I'm pretty sure word got back to them Tron came back.

That time was the last time we went over there, we couldn't keep going back it was a waste of time so I let it go. Me, Divine, and Star was on our way to Manhattan one night and I ran into Iesha on Gates, so we talked for a minute. I hadn't seen her in a long time. She asked why I hadn't come to see my daughter in the hospital... I said I didn't know I had a daughter. She gave me her number so we could hook up and I could see my daughter. I was excited that next day, and I told my mother and my sister I had a daughter. I called Iesha and asked when I could see my daughter. She said I didn't tell you? She died in the hospital. That's when I realized this girl had been lying the whole time. She was never pregnant to begin with. I offered her money the night before... Now I see why she didn't take it. Even though I knew she was a liar, I still had feelings for her. She started talking to this kid on the next block and I just happened to be at the park with my man Ug face, and her new man was there kissing all over another chick. I went back and told her for two reasons: one I still wanted her back and two I wanted to rub it in her face.

But as far as the hood went, I definitely violated by telling her that. I was with Mark and my nephew Chris; I told her then left the block. By the time I got to the corner he came behind me and said something slick, so I told him yeah I told her. He swung and grazed me, so we threw up our hands in the street, the dude picked up a bottle and tried to bust me with it and missed, so I said alright you're gonna pick up stuff. I'm not gonna fight you. I had plans to kill him. I went down the street to Kev's house; he gave me a bulletproof vest, latex gloves, and a burner. Me and Suicide was going to do a drive by. It was so many dudes on that block that you couldn't just walk down there and shoot somebody without a bunch of guns blazing at you, so I was gonna hang out the window on him. Me and Suicide was waiting on T-Lo (his best friend) to come back with the stolen car. Iesha and some girl came to me trying to get me to squash the beef, saying, "You can't take a loss?" she thought he busted me in the head with that bottle but it missed.

I said yeah I can take a loss, but I'm going to kill your man. She begged and pleaded with me not to take it any further. The only thing that messed up my plans was T-Lo not coming back with the stolen car. I figured If I don't get him then he's gonna get me either way it's beef. But Lil Will, a short guy from the block who was well known for that gunplay saw the kid I had beef with and told him to squash it. Lil Will wasn't a fighter at all, but he would shoot you and everybody knew it. The kid I had the beef with told some murderers that I said I was going to kill them when I see them. So every time I was gone off the block they came through looking for me. But when I hung on the block all day long nobody came through. He knew he couldn't come on my block for me so he set me up with some dudes who could. In every hood, every projects, and every block, there is rank and order.

Me and Troy was on the corner one day, and the kid I had beef with jumped out of a car in the middle of the street with another kid. So I thought it was on, but he came to me and squashed the beef like Lil Will told him to. I shook his hand and we dead it right there. A few weeks later some of us were on Greene Avenue, when some kids across the street started mouthing off. We went on the block and grabbed those hammers and went back. It was about 10 of us and everybody was packing. We spotted the kids in front of the Police station and we were gonna shoot them right there. They went and got the kid I had the beef with. Lil Will was telling the kid you know how I get down, but he was begging Will to let it go. Those kids were about to get it right there in front of 79th precinct. After Lil Will talked to the kid and his soldiers, we went back down the block and put those guns away. Back on Gates avenue, Stevie Nicks and Shawn Boogie was playing with a hammer (a real one) and it flew off the handle hitting Stevie Nicks in the head.

He started bleeding and Shawn Boogie was so nervous he asked us what was the number to 911? One thing I liked about the Rebels that was different from my Lexington Ave. crew was that they didn't hug the block. We were all over Manhattan every single day. Divine took us to some expensive club that had a real long line on the outside and told security to tell the DJ that Divine is here. Security went in and came back out and said y'all can come in. Believe me, that security guard didn't go to that DJ but it worked out fine. We would hit a lot of Caucasian clubs in Manhattan and get them for their money because they automatically assumed we were drug dealers... I wonder why. The club would be so packed we would beat them on this side and go chill on the other side. Who were they going to tell, the police? We went to a lesbian bar one night and I saw this gorgeous girl sitting with her friend (who was the man in the relationship) when she got up and went to the bar for drinks I headed to the table to talk to her girl. She wouldn't give me any play; she was committed to her lesbian friend. I hurried up and got up before her friend got back to the table. Every time she went to the bar I went and sat at her table.

She said to me later "you think I don't see you trying to talk to my girl?" And a few weeks later she was on Ricki Lake with another girl. We left there and went to the 50 cent hot dog place in the village where we met Guru from Gang Starr; we kicked it with him for a while and drunk beer with him. He wasn't the scary type; he was comfortable around us like he knew us for years. Suicide came through the block one night and asked me to ride with him to Clinton Hills. Suicide was a white boy on the outside but he was black on the inside. He was a professional car thief. I was walking down the street with him one day and he got in a car faster than a person with a key, no exaggeration. He brought the car back later and was mad because he couldn't park it in the same spot. That night I went to Clinton Hills with him and he told me the plan. We were gonna catch a ride back to Bed Stuy and rob the cab driver. He picked up a trash bag off the street to fool the cab driver into thinking we was legit. The cab driver popped the trunk and Suicide put the garbage he found on the street in there.

We got back to Bed Stuy, and Sui handed me the slap jack and I waited till we got in front of PS 25 and slapped him hard on the side of his head. The cabby started yelling and screaming, and then he jumped out and stopped a city bus. We were in the back seat trying to get our doors open and Sui jumped out the driver door. I was still in the back seat trying to open my door when I turned around and saw that the bus driver opened the doors. I hopped across the seat and took off running down Marcus Garvey behind Sui. I ran and didn't stop until I made it to Lexington and Throop. Me and Stacy was on the prowl one night and met two Puerto Rican girls who lived near Fulton. They invited us up to their house. Stacy went in the bedroom with the prettiest one and I didn't bother the other one. She knew I wasn't really interested so she went to her room and went to sleep. I fell asleep on the living room couch. Stacy woke up in the middle of the night and said let's go. I saw a bunch of money sitting on the living room table, so we took all of it and got up out of there.

We laughed about that all the way back to the Ave. I was still doing my thing on the block; I would come outside 7:00am every morning and start hustling. I couldn't understand why people were going to work when we could all get this fast money. Some crack head owed me money, so her and her husband went and told my mother I was selling drugs. I would try to work with some of the fiends and let them pay me back on the first but then I found out I had to run some of them down. One crack head I knew never came with money, she always came with clothes. She had reasonable prices, her shirts and jeans were always on point. She always got rid of her stuff on our block. Around this time I was paying for a room in the crack house, two crack heads owned it, a brother and a sister. They really tried to extort me for more and more crack in order to stay there. They were cool for a while but as their habit got worse and worse, they demanded more and more. One night the whole block jumped them. We beat them like they stole something, the woman and her brother. We unofficially officially took over the crack house.

The D's (detectives) came through one night looking for guns but none of us had any weapons on us. One of my boys had a bag full of crack in his jacket and the D's gave him all his crack back. All the crack he had in that bag would have gotten him double digits in a prison cell. If the D's came looking for guns and you had crack they used to give it back, but if they came looking for crack and you had a gun you were going for a ride down the street. It was about a year later and Clarence who taught me the game and said don't sell to anyone you don't know. But he didn't follow his own rule. Me and him were on the steps of the crack house one day and this Spanish guy walked up and said "you got anything?" I said I don't know what you're talking about. Here goes greedy, wanting to hurry up and finish his packages said, "I got something!" and while he was making the sell there was a suspicious looking white guy at the corner on the pay phone. Once he made that sell this crack head ran up the block and said that's the D's on the corner.

I stepped out the yard and started walking; I didn't have to run, because they didn't have anything on me. When she said that, a van pulled around the corner real fast and bagged him. The same guy who taught me the game didn't follow the rules. The block was hot; the police knew what was going on. I stood on the block and told all those Jamaicans that if I get locked up and they didn't try to get me out they were coming with me. Something like that is supposed to get you killed; you don't make threats like that. One Jamaican said, "You know no one is going to give you work any more right?" I said I don't care. I went and bought my own work. I got a crack head to make a run for me and pick up my vials and my tops. I bought the same color tops the Jamaicans had so I could stand at the corner and catch their customers and it worked. I didn't leave the block. I pumped all day and all night. I had shorty Val running to the pizza shop for me and tipped him lovely so I wouldn't miss any money.

The Jamaicans went to my man Black one day and told him I was pumping my own work and Black sided with the Jamaicans and asked me to stop since all of them already had their work on the block. That was our block. We were supposed to get rid of the Jamaicans, and they didn't even live on Lexington. They just came around to make money and leave. So it wouldn't be any problem between me and Black, I stopped pumping my work after I finished my package. My sister told me, our mother was moving down south and I should ask her if I could go with her. My mother lived around the corner from me and we weren't on speaking terms. But I went around there and asked her if I could move to South Carolina with her to change my life, and she said yes. This other drug dealer that gave me some work started looking for me because I kept the money and the drugs. He was looking for me every day, and I was looking right at him through the window. I just needed to stall a few more weeks until I could move down south.

I moved in with my mother at this time while we were waiting to move to South Carolina and homeboy came by day and night ringing that bell looking for his money and drugs. The night before leaving New York, I was on the corner hanging with Black and the crew and Black knew I was leaving for South Carolina so he told me he flipping on Shock and Grimey tonight (two brothers)... You with us? I said whatever. It was about 15 of us on the corner that night. And while we were standing there, Shock and Grimey drove by us and parked on our block. We walked down there to the middle of the block where they were and everybody started swinging. I didn't jump in; that night for some reason I had a heart. I felt like they were outnumbered and didn't want any part in it. After the brutal beat down session everybody went bowling except for me and Divine. We went and hung out on the corner of Greene and Throop. All of a sudden I see Shock and Grimey in the distance coming our way. Both of them was holding their jackets and I knew they were packing because nobody comes back unless they're packing.

As they got close to us Divine walked up to them to cop a plea. He was kind of tipsy. So Grimey smacked Divine, he stumbled and his hat fell off. When I saw that I ran up on Shock and Grimey about to swing on both of them. That's when they turned around and pointed their guns at me. I opened my arms wide and said shoot. At that point in life I don't think I really cared anymore. They put their guns back in their jacket and walked off. I went back on the block and destroyed Shock's car after that. He's trying to go to war with us with his car parked on our block. I took a bat and busted out all his windows. The next day we were on our way to South Carolina, and I never turned back.

CHAPTER EIGHT

Moving Down South

January 1997. The Big Apple was in the distance and I felt like I was leaving my past behind and starting fresh. I wanted something I never really wanted before: a job. I knew moving to South Carolina would take some adjusting. It's a big difference between visiting for the summer and living there. I only told a few peeps in New York that I was leaving and others heard it through the street. Me and Tasha came first, and my mother left like a week or two later. She didn't have enough money to come too, so she stayed behind. To this day I have never been back to New York. I have been offered free trips and turned every one of them down. I had a bunch of great memories there, but when I think of New York, I see a dark cloud. I do miss a few people, but I mostly miss the food. Hot dogs off the street, Jamaican Beef Patties, and Pizza. The first couple of months in South Carolina weren't easy at all. I was used to coming outside and seeing everyone right there, but now when I come out and see trees and houses down the road. The worst part was trying to get around and get out looking for a job.

We had some cousins in Clio, South Carolina that would come and take us to fill out applications sometimes. My sister used to go to different clubs with my cousin Aaron, but I would stay in the house and chill. No buses, no trains, no corner store, no New York. I was bored out of my mind; this place was a retirement home for real. I found out my man Black was locked up on Riker's Island so I wrote him a letter that started off like Nas' "One Love". "What up kid, I know things are rough doing your bid" For a long time I didn't want to speak to anyone in New York because I didn't want to find out anyone was dead. Especially after finding out that Derrick (Troy's nephew) was killed. I use to ride with my mother, my Uncle, and his wife just to get out of the house on Saturdays. I was riding with my Uncle one day when he told me he saw on the news a rapper was murdered but he didn't know who it was. Later that day I found out it was Notorious B.I.G. That really hurt because Biggie was from Bed Stuy.

Jay Z was from Bed Stuy too, but Biggie was our voice. That news was unreal and heartbreaking, and the type of news I use to try to avoid. Before Biggie came out and blew up he was supposed to put my man Fred on, and Fred was going to turn around and put me on. But when Big came out with Juicy and skyrocketed to success we never heard from Big. My cousin got me a little part-time job at Gailey and Lord on the weekends. A full time job would have been better, but anything beats a blank.

I would go over there and work with the cleanup crew. My job was to scrape machines and remove all the build-up on them. It was just a Saturday and Sunday job, for cigarette and beer money. I went to hang out with Jimmy and another guy at the Knife and Fork, just to get out the house for a little while. I was mostly listening to music and drinking while they were kicking it with different people.

When it came to dudes I was anti-social, but when it came to girls my middle name was "shorty what's up?" As we left, I spotted a girl that I wanted to talk to, so I stepped to her and kicked it for a hot second before getting her number. Her name was Angela. She had a North Carolina number, but I still reached out. I was never the type to call the same day and seem thirsty; I would always wait 2 days. We hit it off and started talking on the phone every day. I was embarrassed to tell her that I had a weekend job so I lied and acted as if I was at work all week long. Jim Ford was going to North Carolina one day so I caught a ride over there with him to see her. That first visit to her house wasn't a good visit. She had a girl over there that wouldn't leave and wouldn't let us talk. She was a third wheel of the worst kind. I walked to the store and grabbed me something to sip on with my beer and cigarette money.

I came back to her house and continued on with me, her, and the third wheel. Wheel of Fortune came on and I thought I was very good at Wheel of Fortune until I met third wheel. This girl figured out every single puzzle. Angela and I didn't really talk that much on that visit. I got my brother and Linda to take me back over there the next week and this time we were alone.

We sat on the couch and just laughed and joked for a while, I was shocked that the third wheel wasn't around. Some guy came over looking for her roommate, but the roommate wasn't home and he took it upon himself to take a seat.

I'm from Brooklyn. I'm not crazy, and the roommate thing didn't really fly with me, but she wasn't my girl and it wasn't my place to check anyone. He sat around for 5 minutes acting as if he was waiting around on the roommate then he left. Shortly after I left too when my ride got back. Me and my brother would get together and get cases of beer and sometimes weed. I wasn't really a weed smoker; I was more of a drinker. Riding and drinking was all I wanted to do. At times my brother was cool then other times he acted funny because of Linda. She would wear more than one face. Sometime she loved his family and other times didn't want him around his family. It was really breaking my mother's heart and my brother lived right down the road and acted like he didn't know her sometimes. Linda use to go to the house of a root worker to sit around and talk. They took me there one time and we drunk creek liquor. So we wondered was she paying the woman to keep him around. There was a period where he stopped coming around us altogether on her orders.

I couldn't believe it. There ain't that much love in the world. That took me back to one of my South Carolina visits; my brother and Linda came to New York and begged me to come back with them so I did. One day while both of them was at work, her mother who was racist told Linda I cursed her out over the phone and she made me leave her house. My brother didn't say a word; I didn't even see him try to say a word. She kicked me out her house while we were having a cook-out. Everybody was saying "your brother's wrong!" Johnny who I knew from Brooklyn took me to his house for a while and let me call my mother to tell her I need money to come back, and she told me to go to an aunt's house. Johnny felt bad for me and gave me a few dollars. Everyone else was saying man, if he can do that to his own brother... Real shame. But it was obvious he was still in that same stronghold from 5 years ago. Feelings started growing between me and Angela, so she asked me to move in with her and her 3-year-old daughter, so I did.

CHAPTER NINE

Moving To North Carolina

I moved in with Angela and her daughter and we were having a ball. I started meeting people, mostly her family and friends she grew up with. Neither one of us had a car so we depended on other people for everything. She had one friend that was real cool, Dee; everybody loved her, from guys to girls. Her sense of humor was ridiculous. I filled out applications here and there and nobody called. I went to a temporary agency and put an application in and still nothing. Angela got a call back before I did and she started working first. I'd get up in the morning and put her daughter on the bus. Most of the time her hair needed a little touch up so I would slap some gel on it and brush it. Her daughter was 4 years old and knew everybody's business. She could tell you who was dating who and cheating on whom. She told me one night her mother and Dee went to see some guys. I never asked Angela about the stuff she told me, thinking maybe she didn't understand the reason they were there. She was very spoiled, and would cry for hours. I timed her one day just to see how long she would cry, and she cried for 6 hours straight.

She'd cry for any and every reason. If you told her to sleep in her own bed, she cried. If you told her to go play, she cried. That one really confused me, because growing up we cried when we couldn't go play, and here she is crying because she's being told to go play. One hot summer day me and Angela walked to the grocery store to pick up a few things. We loaded up on groceries and needed a ride back home so we called a cab. We put all the stuff in the trunk of the cab and headed back to the house. I made a little joke in the back seat about beating the cab driver up. I thought I was whispering but the cabby heard what I said so he called the police and told them to meet him at our house. When the cops got there, the cab driver didn't say anything about what I was saying in the back seat, he told them I put a scratch on the cab the size of a dime. I couldn't believe this guy.

What really shocked me was when the cop said do you want him arrested and he said yes. I thought I was going home to have my favorite meal, spaghetti, but instead I'm in the back seat of a cop car on my way to jail. I got to the holding cell and saw a bunch of dudes that looked like they were home. There wasn't anywhere for me to lie down and I was so tired. I spoke to Angela that night and she told me she was working on getting me out. The next day she posted my bail and got me out of there but I still had to go to court. I had me a court-appointed lawyer who felt she could get me out of this without paying a dime. The charge was injury to personal property and they wanted $260 for a scratch that was already on the cab. The cab driver never tried to call the police until he heard what I said. So how are you calling police for a scratch on the cab? When did you notice the scratch when you never got out the cab? They set me up.

They told the judge "we want Mr. Moses thrown back in jail your honor because he's from New York and he's a flight risk." I heard it all at that point. I'm going to go on the run out of state because they scratched their own cab? In the court room the cab driver and the owner (both Caucasian) would look at me with hate in their eyes. We went back and forth to court a total of three times before the judge threw out the case. They also included that I was barred from riding in their cabs, which didn't matter to me at all. As long as I didn't have to pay $260 for something I didn't do. Angela and I would ride out with different friends of hers and hit different clubs. One night we went to a hole in the wall in Maxton, NC and there was a girl in there half-drunk taking off her clothes. I tried to be a good boyfriend and not look. I ended up getting a job in Maxton, at Maxton Meats. I enjoyed the job at first because it was my first official job. In New York I did a lot of painting and moving furniture, all off the books. In that plant they made hot dogs, Vienna sausages, and we had chicken.

While I worked there, I couldn't eat any of that stuff because I got to see the process. I was on 2nd shift working 4:00pm to 12:00am. What I hated most about that job was you never knew when you were getting off. We had to stay until the order was finished. One night 3rd shift came in and stayed in the canteen their whole shift while we worked until 1st shift came back. It was more money, but I didn't want to work that long. I would ride to work with my supervisor who only charged me $20 a week and he packed up that little car. We were in that car literally laying on each other. We were so cramped up in there that when you finally got to your house, you had to do a 5 minute stretch before you walked in the door to get the feeling back in your arms and legs. The USDA man shut us down for all the chicken lying around on the floor and everybody had to clean up. Here's where riding with the supervisor was a bad idea. I stood on the wall while everyone was cleaning up talking to about 7 other guys, which was wrong. My supervisor came out of nowhere and said "Tron, why you aren't cleaning up?" I didn't mind him saying that, but you don't see these other guys I'm standing next to?

He was scared to say something to them and only picked me out because I rode with him. One day I got to work at 4:00pm and around 4:07 I walked right back out, I quit. I started walking down the road and didn't know how I was going to get to the house and bumped into someone who knew Angela. Her daughter was with one of her sisters so we went and got a hotel room to hang out and relax and have access to the pool and everything. I heard her on the phone with her sister telling her to bring her daughter to the hotel. I was like if all three of us are going to be together we might as well have stayed home, so I left. I used to hang out with her aunt who lived next door and drink beer, Angela didn't drink. I needed a drinking partner. Her aunt was cool, she came over one day while Angela was at work and taught me how to fry chicken that I passed off as my own. Me and Angela started having problems and weren't getting along too well. I started physically abusing her when I got mad. Whenever we would have an argument, I would let it build up to that point and then I'd start hitting her.

Then when I calmed down, I would apologize to her and tell her I would never hit her again. Her mother talked to me one day and said if I'm going to hit her then don't hit her in the face. I said ok. My mother even spoke to me on the phone and said "Tron, stop hitting that girl, you're over there around her whole family," but I didn't care. She made me mad one day so I punched her in the face, and she picked up a big frying pan and hit me in the head with it. Another time we got into it and had a fall out, she pulled a blade and sliced me across the leg. I had a real big open wound. She got on the phone and called the ambulance and even gave me a story to tell them. She said tell them you cut your leg on the bed spring, and like an idiot, I did. They took me to the hospital and I got some stitches but the Doctor who stitched me wasn't buying the bed spring story.

He said he always got guys in there on a Friday night who got into an altercation with their girlfriends and get cut. After she cut me I didn't hit her no more, now when she made me mad I went for a walk. I started working at a convenience store not too far from the house and probably worked there a few months. When we would be low on food or anything, my boss would let me get what we needed until pay day. One day it was drizzling, so he offered me a ride home, but I figured out later that he just wanted to see where I lived at. Another time it was raining real hard and he didn't offer me a ride. One night while at work the police came to the store for me and said I pulled Angela's weave out her head. This time I was innocent; I didn't lay a hand on her but of course they're going to side with the woman. I spent the night in jail and got out the next day. I still had to go to court for that situation but with her not showing up for court they threw it out. Our relationship would be good for a few days and then we'd be at odds again.

Looking back now, we knew it wasn't working but neither one of us wanted to let go. And a lot of people are in relationships like that now; they know it isn't working, they don't see a future in it; because they don't want to be alone ,they stay in a dead relationship. I realized in my own life that I always settled because I never really believed that I could have what I want. I knew it was good women out there but I thought so low of myself that I didn't think I deserved one. In our case I'm not just saying that I settled; we both settled. A man is not going to cheat on a woman that has his heart and he's happy with, I don't care what they tell you. But anyway, her and one of her girlfriends went to bingo one day and I was supposed to go pick up her daughter from another family member's house but I never went. I went and hung out at another one of her cousin's house. They had a cousin come over there to visit and I was feeling a little nice off the beer so I started kicking it with her. She said I thought you and Angela was together, I said nah we just roommates.

So me and the cousin left that cousin's house and went back to Angela house. We got in me and Angela's bed and had sex a few times. Then all of a sudden I heard a car pull up outside, it was Angela. I jumped up real fast and told the girl to grab her clothes and she ran to the other side of the trailer to Angela's daughter's room. I went to the bathroom and locked the door. Angela knew something was up because we didn't lock the door when we went to the bathroom. She headed for her daughter's room to see if I picked her up and before she got there the girl yelled out, "Did she leave yet?" She messed up when she did that. Angela turned back and grabbed a knife from the kitchen and started beating on her cousin and cutting her. She chased that girl down the street doing damage. And while all this was going on it was some neighbors outside sitting down and I overheard one of them say, I knew that was going to happen.

When Angela came back to the house, I thought I was about to get cut too. But she was crying and told me to pack my stuff she's taking me back to my mother house. She cried all the way to Blenheim, and I sat in the passenger seat, cold and heartless. I blamed her for my cheating on her. I was so cold towards her that whole ride and she was doing me a favor by taking me home because most women wouldn't have done it. Most of you women reading this wouldn't have done it. She dropped me off and went her way. After a few days I started missing her and realizing that I was wrong. My family was having a cook-out in the country and I called and invited her and her daughter. They came and I apologized to her and told her it would never happen again. We talked back and forth on the phone and I would come over and visit. After a while she came and got me and I moved back in. I got a job at Campbell Soup in Maxton, NC. I loved it there. The pay wasn't great at all for a temp, but it was one of my favorite jobs. I didn't have to buy lunch if I didn't want to because I would get food from all the cooks. If they were making something I liked, I went and got a can from them.

I use to hang with this girl Lachonda every day at work, everybody thought we were dating but we were just cool. She was from Kings County (Brooklyn) as well and that's how we bonded. It was a bunch of people on the job from Brooklyn, The Bronx, Harlem, and other places. One day it was about 10 of us sitting at the table talking and found out that everyone was from New York. I had just met Marisa, this Spanish girl from the Bronx. After work we were standing outside talking, waiting on our rides. I thought she was attractive but I wasn't hitting on her, it was just conversation. 3rd shift was walking up to the building while we were talking and her boyfriend blended in the crowd and jumped out on her. He got out the car and saw us talking and automatically assumed we were kicking it so he crept in the crowd. He grabbed her up and started choking on her. I just stood there watching because where I'm from you didn't mind other people business. Her boyfriend had some cousins who worked there that came outside and pulled him off her, he never said anything to me so I didn't say anything to him.

They started giving me overtime and I would go in 4 hours early. Everybody was hating on me because they wanted overtime and couldn't get it. I didn't look for it; it came looking for me. I use to converse with this guy at work every day and didn't know at the time he was my first cousin from Clio, South Carolina. I never asked him where he was from or who his family was? We just talked about work and girls. Shortly after, I started selling weed in the plant. I sold one bag to a girl that was my next-door neighbor and she was telling people at work, so I was making extra money on the job. I was servicing 1st and 2nd shift every day. The people at work were becoming more and more like a family and started hanging out on the weekends. Some smoked weed and others would drink, but we all clicked. Angela even thought I was seeing Lachonda and I tried to tell her I wasn't. One night while we were all sitting together at Lachonda's house, and Angela came over. I let her in and said see, that's her man right there. The dude and Lachonda was dating, but he later told me when he heard me say that to Angela, he said to himself, "I ain't her man." He might not have been claiming her, but they sure looked like a couple to me. Around this time Angela got back her tax money and bought her first car.

She would be gone all the time and her friend Dee used to joke and say she had a man, I didn't think nothing of it. It really didn't bother me that she stayed gone because we got along better like that. If she wasn't working she stayed gone. I popped her daughter one day and the girl's father came over there with his gun but wouldn't get out the car. Dee went up to the car and he sat the gun on his lap so she could tell me she seen it. Tony dated Angela's oldest sister, and me and him used to hang sometimes. I wouldn't use the word friend. He talked about fighting all the time and I never could stand those types. I plotted one night with him to take Angela's car when she fell asleep and we could go hit this party. She was a hard sleeper. You could rob her house, and she wouldn't wake up. I had him meet me down the road and I went down there and got him. When I pulled up, he wouldn't get in the car so I took off and went to the party without him. When I got back that night Angela told me how Tony doubled back and knocked on the door to tell her I took the car. I said to myself "alright, I'm going to get him back for that, it's just a matter of time." When I saw him I never let on that I knew what he did; I just played it cool.

One day my opportunity for payback came. The family was talking about a missing picture. It was of one of the sisters (4 sisters) in a bathing suit and Tony told me that he had the picture. So while they were standing there talking about it I said that Tony had it. It was like a day or two later when Tony and the oldest sister came by the house and he asked me in front of everyone if I said he had the picture. He was assuming that I was gonna back down and change my story, because he always talked about fighting but that was never my conversation. When I said "yeah you took it," and he swung on me and hit me in the eye. When he did that, I found out the person who talked about fighting all the time was just mouth. After he caught me in the eye that was the last punch he got and I worked on him for like 5 minutes. I wasn't into repeating what people told me, but I wanted to get even with him. I didn't consider us friends but I did feel we were cooler than that. After that day I never had a problem out of him again. I started thinking about life and wanted to settle down, so I went and bought Angela an engagement ring.

I showed the ring to some people I knew before I popped the question. I was ready to make that step and go all the way with us. I was excited and couldn't wait to ask her. I got down on one knee and I popped the question and she said yes. I was being faithful because I thought I had a good woman and didn't want to lose her. At this point it was over 2 years since I physically abused her, and that was behind us. No woman deserves to be beat up by a man, so when we didn't agree I just walked away. Things were going great for us; we were finally on our way until one day her mother came by. She walked in the house and told Angela she needed to speak to her. It looked like it was very serious. I couldn't hear what they were talking about but I soon found out. Angela's daughter told the grandmother that I touched her inappropriately. Just when it seemed like everything was going right it was still going wrong. A parent should believe their child, but when she asked me and I said NO, I felt she should have taken my word.

Once again, I was headed back to my mother's house. Angela called a ride to take me because something was wrong with her car. Her and the girl were in the front while I was in the back devastated. The only reason she rode with us because she was afraid me and the girl would hook up. But hooking up was the furthest thing from my mind. I was just dealt a serious blow. I didn't even look at children inappropriately nor have a desire to touch them. About a week went by and DSS got involved in the whole thing. They questioned her daughter for about an hour and found out that family members told her to say that. I was glad my name was cleared but I knew this time I was never going back. What if someone would have taken the law into their own hands and came to the house to murder me?

CHAPTER TEN

My Appointed Time

I did get back with Angela after that, but I didn't move back in. I would go over there and spend the night or maybe a couple of days here and there but that was it. I didn't want to be put in a worse situation than that. I started working at Marlboro Park Hospital and was putting some money aside for a rainy day. She would come over and visit me when she could, mostly on my payday. It took a while before I figured that one out. I was in North Carolina hanging out with her when she had to take some guy to work. I wasn't the jealous type so I didn't have a problem with her taking him to work. This turned out to be the same guy that Dee joked about earlier and said she was seeing. I found out later on that they really were seeing each other and Dee told me but she put it in the form of a joke. I came to visit her unannounced one day and she wasn't home, so I went by one of her cousin's house and she hadn't seen her.

One of Angela's sisters came over and told me she was on a trip with a truck driver. And while we were still sitting there another sister came in and said the same thing, and then her niece. I felt bad that I did her wrong, but now I guess it was payback. I spent the night at the cousin's house on the couch and called Angela the next morning and she picked up the phone. I said "so you're taking trips with truck drivers now?" She said it was her vagina (that's not the word she used), she can do what she wants with it. I walked over there to the house and she let me in. I grabbed my engagement ring off the VCR and headed towards the door. She got on the phone to call the cops and I knew they would reach me before I made it back to the cousin's house so I took the ring and threw it at her. I never contacted her again, I moved on with my life. But what goes around definitely comes back around. The guy she cheated on me with started beating on her. I saw her one day and both of her eyes were messed up. I felt bad for her. There was nothing I could do to help her. We went our separate ways in the year 2000.

I was no longer working at Marlboro Park Hospital, I started working at Marley's. After only a week of having the job I messed up big time. I was hanging out all night drinking and when I looked at the time, it was time to go to work. So I caught a ride to work still smelling like alcohol and everything. I told the girl that was over me to tell the supervisor I didn't feel good so I could go home. That wasn't what she told him, because I was called to the office. He asked me a bunch of crazy questions, trying to fill me out and I knew he smelled the alcohol. He took some kind of report that was read back to me the next week. He said I was in the office high as a kite and kept staring at the ceiling. I was feeling good, but I wasn't watching a ceiling. They let me keep my job but I think they were watching me and it never happened again. I eventually got off 2nd shift and went to first, and they made me a forklift driver against my will. But it turned out they did me a favor because I got a chance to go outside and smoke when I was ready. I made more money off side hustles there then I did from the actual job.

I sold CDs, ringtones, preaching videos, sex toys, and I blew up pictures for people. We worked from 6:00am to 2:30pm. From the time I got home all the way to 4:00 or 5:00 in the morning I was getting people's orders ready, then I'd catch a nap before work. I didn't care about sleep; I had to get that money and I did. I wasn't only making a name for myself for the merchandise I was selling, but also for being a player. Whenever a new girl would start working there, they would warn her about me. I found that out while sitting at the house of one of the girls they warned, so I guess it didn't work. Goody came to me one day and told me a new girl is telling people on the line that I was going to be hers. I said to tell her I'm not interested. She wasn't ugly, she just looked rough. The girl saw me in the canteen and while standing at the soda machines she said real loud, "I don't like broke N....a's anyway" so I guess I did us both a favor.

My sister had already been going to church and had given her life to the Lord, and she had a friend she wanted to witness to me. Instead of witnessing to me, she was trying to holla at me. She was a nice looking female, and we would talk on the phone daily. She came by the house one day and we sat in the living room kissing and she told me how she thinks I'd be great in bed.

But it never ever reached that point. When she left the house that day, I never answered her phone calls again. She was nice looking, she was interesting, she was cool, but she was supposed to be saved. And here I am a sinner feeling guilt for touching her. If you knew me at that time you'd know there wasn't anyone but God for me to turn her down. She called me every day all day for weeks but I wouldn't pick up the phone; God blocked it. And I'm not even saying He did it for me, I believe He did that for her sake. Every day after work I smoked a bag of weed and drunk 2 forties of Old English, that was my routine.

This woman at work used to call me Jonah. She said I was running from the Lord and told me I won't see death until I tell the Lord yes. In 2004 I couldn't miss any more days, and I was out for a few days because of pain in my foot. I took a Doctor's note back but they didn't accept the note and fired me. When they got rid of me things got worse; I started really drinking bad. All I wanted to do was drink morning, noon, and night. I use to go in AOL chat rooms and converse with different people on there and one day I saw where this guy said he was from Bed Stuy, so I sent him a message trying to find out if we knew the same people. It turned out he lived around the corner from where I used to live on Quincy. He told me he knew Dave and a bunch of other people I knew. I asked him how was Mya from Gates doing?

He said Mya resting in peace, and I was sorry to hear that. I would also converse with this girl on there from somewhere in North Carolina. She seemed cool. We sent each other pictures and she was a pretty Spanish girl. We traded numbers and started talking on the phone and I asked her to come see me and hang out and she did. The night she came she couldn't find my house so I walked to the top of the road to meet her. The car pulled up next to me and I got in it. It was a girl in the driver seat and one in the passenger seat. I assumed the girl in the passenger seat that I was sitting behind was her, because the girl in the driver seat was way bigger than the girl in the pictures. She introduced herself and the girl riding shot gun. That's when I realized she had been sending me fake pictures. I didn't want to be rude but she talked to me like I didn't notice she had been sending me fake pictures. We rode uptown they wanted to get some drinks and I was still in shock. They saw the knife and fork, which is a night club, was open and wanted to go over there but I was embarrassed to take her over there so I said no, they be killing people over there.

Before they came to Blenheim to get me, they got a hotel room at the Marlboro Inn. As we pulled up to the hotel, I told them to go in. I'm about to run over here to Sav Way and grab some beer. I went in Sav Way and called me a ride. Then I dipped out of Sav Way and walked over to the Shell store. It turns out they never went in the hotel; they parked over on a side street and watched me while I was in Sav Way. Then they came to the Shell store too and the girl riding shot gun came in. I still could not believe this girl didn't even try to explain those pictures to me as if I wouldn't notice. She called my phone while I was in the store and I wouldn't answer. She was sitting right there looking at me. She was on my voice mail cursing me out and telling me how I'm not all that. Maybe not, but I sent her my real pictures.

My cousin came and picked me up and we laughed about it all the way back to the country. I guess you can't win them all.

It seemed like 2004 was the worst year of my life. I was losing everything but my mind. I even tried sniffing coke one time but didn't get anything out of it so I never tried again. I was at a store in Bennettsville one day and two guys asked my cousin to step outside, they were about to jump him. They didn't know he was my cousin because we weren't even together. When they went outside I went right with them and stood in the midst of the conversation. Now it's even, what's up? They wanted to talk nice then. My cousin was so shook up, so he started talking extra nice to me. I started seeing this new girl who I met through one of my brother's friends. It wasn't anything serious because I couldn't see myself trusting her. She was cool for a hot minute and then we fell out for a reason I don't even remember. I was riding with my man Jeremy one night and we stopped at Clark's pool room for a hot minute. I got out and passed like 6 or 7 guys in a huddle, they were convincing him to shoot. I went and stood in the door. I looked at the bar to see if I knew anyone over there and then I looked at the pool table, and that's when a guy came running past me and fell on the floor and was trying to get back up. Another guy came and stood shoulder to shoulder with me shooting him while he was on the floor.

We were so close that I could have knocked the gun out of his hand, but I froze. The kid on the floor was dead from all the gunshot wounds. It was about 50 witnesses to the murder. Every day I was going home with hangovers and I was getting tired of being a drunk. I was starting to hate my life. One morning I got up and said to the Lord, "God please put it in my heart for me to come to you!" Even though that prayer was sincere and from the heart, I forgot all about what I prayed because I went back out and did the same thing, I had no self-control. A couple of weeks later, my sister who was already saved called me while I was at my brother's house to give me a message. She said, "God told me to tell you to get ready!" I was at my brother's house drinking and having a ball; I didn't want to hear that. That prayer I prayed must have reached the throne room. I hurried up and got off the phone with her so I could get back to business. I was over her house one day and sitting in the living room alone and for some reason I was watching Paula White talking about sowing seeds.

I felt the Lord tugging on my heart. I only had three cigarettes left in my pack and enough money in my pocket to get another one. But when Paula got done preaching, I gave my sister everything in my pocket to put in the offering plate. I didn't understand at the moment I was hearing God speak to me, and I was sowing towards my deliverance. My sister would call me every Sunday and ask me if I was going to church and I would say no. After a while I just started ignoring her calls on Sunday. One day I told her in the middle of the week that I would go, but by the time Sunday got here the devil snatched it. I honestly did mean it when I said it. From the time I prayed that prayer to the time my sister called me at my brother's house was about 2 weeks. From the time of that phone call to the time I gave God a YES for real was about 4 or 5 weeks. I got tired of running; I wanted to be free, I wanted to live a saved life, so I told God yes! Immediately all the weight and burdens I was carrying begin to fall off me. I felt like a new creature in Christ. Everyone I owed money to that I never planned on paying back, I went and gave them their money.

I didn't care about money because what I found was so much better than that. I told everyone I knew about what the Lord did for me. I started reading the Bible every day, just desiring to know Him. I just wanted Jesus, and it's 10 years later and I still want Jesus. I wasn't going to church for the first couple of weeks of my salvation; I stayed at home. My sister asked me to come with her, but I told her no because I owed one of the members at her church money and I didn't have it. She mentioned it to him and he said "Tell your brother to come." He played a role in where I am today, because had he been angry with me and responded differently I probably wouldn't have stood this long. You can't stay home and think you're strong in the Lord; the enemy is the one behind you staying home in the first place. It's a seducing spirit. I thank God for my salvation, and I'm going all the way in Him. I didn't write this to glorify anything I've done in the past or even to be judged now for things I did back then. I wrote this so you could see my life in panoramic view; the good, the bad, the beautiful and the ugly, and see that God still called me.

Even while I was out there messing up and going the wrong way, He had a plan for my life. Since I was saved more than 20 people have come to the Lord. And I'm not boasting at all because I'm just getting started. I pray this book has been a blessing to you and I pray you'll tell others about it so they can be blessed as well. And know that the Lord has something better than the streets. Eyes have not seen, nor ears heard, neither has it entered into the heart of man the things that God has prepared for them that love him (1 Corinthians 2:9). God can save anybody: that drunk, that drug dealer, that crack head, that promiscuous teen, that homosexual, that lesbian, that whoremonger, that liar, that prostitute, that pimp, ANYBODY!! To everyone from the past, if I've ever done anything or said anything to hurt you, I ask you to please forgive me, because I forgive you.

CHAPTER ELEVEN

God's Hand Of Protection

I asked my mother a couple of years ago why that guy was chasing us back in 1978. She said it wasn't anyone chasing us; it was a fire in the building. My sister is two years older than me and has no recollection of this at all. I didn't know it was a fire in the building, but to show you how awesome God is, he revealed to me that was an ANGEL behind us. All my life I thought a man was behind us chasing us, but found it odd that my memory of the man was him being pure white; not Caucasian, but pure white! I kept my eyes on him as he ran behind us trying to figure out why wasn't he able to catch us. Truly God will give His angels charge over thee!!

ABOUT THE AUTHOR

Tron Moses is a well sought after photographer. He will travel to various locations for the client or to get a great shot. He mentors many photographers. He has photographed famous people. Tron started photography in 2008. He specializes in Strobist photography which includes portrait and beauty. Tron gives excellent work and has invested in high quality gear guaranteed to satisfy any client. Tron is passionate about every photo. He takes time to retouch and sharpen every image captured on camera. His photography consists of colorful and lively imagery. He is graced to produce outstanding photos for you. He is originally from Brooklyn, New York but currently resides in Bennettsville, South Carolina. In summary, he is a fun guy who loves the art of photography.

www.tronmoses.org

Index

B

Bed Stuy, 7, 12, 15, 17, 31, 55, 61, 79
brother, 2, 4, 6, 8–9, 11, 15–16, 25, 31–33, 36–37, 56, 58, 62–64

C

church, 3–4, 32–34, 79, 82–83
court, 10, 67, 70
cousin, 2–3, 11, 26–27, 31, 38–39, 50, 61, 70–72, 81

D

deliverance, 82
disagreement, 38
disciplinary, 4
Divine, 27, 45, 51, 54, 58–59
drama, 8, 19

F

family, 2, 28, 38–39, 63, 65, 69, 71, 73–74
fighting, 8, 45, 51, 73–74
Fulton, 29–30, 55

G

God, 5, 13, 32–33, 41, 79, 82–85
Greene Avenue, 28, 41, 53

H

Harlem, 15, 72
heart, 3, 6–8, 30–31, 47, 58, 70, 82, 84
homeboys, 32, 58
homeless, 12, 43, 46
hospital, 45, 51–52, 69

J

jail time, 31
job, 9, 33, 42–44, 60–62, 67–68, 72–73, 77–78

L

Lexington, 7, 16, 21, 23, 26–28, 30–31, 34, 41, 54–55, 58
Lord, 32–33, 46, 61, 79, 82–84
love, 4–5, 9, 18, 25, 34, 37–39, 44, 50–51, 63

M

memories, 18, 60, 85
mentor, 32–33
money, 18, 29, 34, 39, 43–44, 48–49, 52, 55–58, 60, 64, 68, 76, 78, 82–83

N

neighbors, 12, 15, 17, 44, 71
New York, 6, 8, 37, 60–61, 63, 67, 72
North Carolina, 62, 65, 76, 80

P

Parables, 34
police, 17, 45, 48–49, 54, 57, 66–67, 70
prayer, 34, 82

Q

Quincy Street, 16, 44

R

relationship, 22, 33, 35, 54, 70

S

school, 8–10, 14, 19–22, 29, 43
South Carolina, 4, 6, 36–37, 58–61, 63
St. Ides, 25, 33
street, 11–12, 15, 21, 26–27, 33, 44, 48, 50, 52–53, 55–56, 60, 71, 84
Suicide, 52, 55

T

Tasha, 3, 5, 7–9, 12, 15, 21, 23–24, 30–32, 41, 60
threats, 8, 22, 45, 57
Throop Avenue, 16

V

VCR, 9, 14, 23, 77
victims, 17, 43

W

witnesses, 32, 79, 82
work, 2, 9, 12, 14, 22, 56–58, 62–63, 68–70, 72–73, 76–79

www.ingramcontent.com/pod-product-compliance
Lightning Source LLC
Chambersburg PA
CBHW071747080526
44588CB00013B/2174